The Merging of Religious and Secular Rule in Tibet

by Dung-dkar blo-bzang 'phrim-las

FOREIGN LANGUAGES PRESS · BEIJING

First Edition   1991
Second Printing   1993

Translated by Chen Guansheng

ISBN 0-8351-2217-4
ISBN 7-119-00672-X

© Foreign Languages Press, Beijing, 1991

Published by Foreign Languages Press
24 Baiwanzhuang Road, Beijing 100037, China

Printed by Beijing Foreign Languages Printing House
19 Chegongzhuang Xilu, Beijing 100044, China

Printed in the People's Republic of China

Contents

Statue of King Srong-btsan
Sgam-po of the Tubo Dynasty.

Statue of Princess Wen Cheng
of the Tang royal house.

Statue of the Buddha brought to Tibet by Princess Wen Cheng.

The Potala Palace standing magnificently at the top of the Red Hill in the city of Lhasa is a sacred centre of Tibetan Buddhism and a treasure house of art. The residence of the highest living Buddha and the seat of the Tibetan local government, it is also a symbol of the merging of religious and secular rule in Tibet.

Khra-'brug Temple, located in Nedong County, is the oldest Buddhist temple in Tibet.

Dga'-ldan Monastery, one of the three major monasteries of the Yellow Sect.

Jokhang Temple, one of the oldest buildings in Tibet, is at the centre of Lhasa.

Bkra-shis-lhun-po (Trashilungpo) Monastery, Panchen Erdeni's "mother monastery," in Gzhis-kha-rtse (Xigaze) is the largest monastery in the Gtsang region.

A mural depicting 'Phags-pa, leader of the Lamaist Sa-skya Sect, at an interview with the Mongol ruler Kublai Khan in 1253. With support from Kublai Khan, 'Phags-pa later held administrative power in Tibet and also became a high official of the Yuan court.

The gold seal of "State Tutor of Murddhabhichikta and King of Expounding Buddhism" granted by the Ming emperor Jia Jing to the Eleventh Phag-mo-grub-pa Sde-srid.

The imperial order issued by the Ming emperor Jia Jing conferring the title of "State Tutor of Murddhabhichikta and King of Expounding Buddhism" upon the Eleventh Phag-mo-grub-pa Sde-srid.

Portrait of the Fifth Dalai Lama.

The Golden Vase and Ivory Tablets given by the Qing emperor were used for deciding the succession of the new Dalai Lama.

The Fifth Dalai Lama at an interview with the Qing Emperor Shun Zhi.

The signing of the "Agreement of the Central People's Government and the Local Government of Tibet on Measures for the Peaceful Liberation of Tibet" on May 23, 1951.

The Tibetan and Han-language texts of the historic agreement which brought about the peaceful liberation of Tibet.

Students of the Academy of Tibetan Buddhism attending a lecture on Buddhist scriptures.

The Grand Prayer Meeting attended by numerous monks at the Jokhang Temple of Lhasa.

I. The Tibetan Regime Before the Establishment of the Politico-Religious Institution and the Rivalries Between Bon and Buddhism in Tibet

1. Bon Religion and Tibetan Society Before the Introduction of Buddhism into Tibet

Everything in the world undergoes changes that start in quantity and end in quality. So was the Tibetan political-religious institution, which developed from a secular power separated from religion into a merger of religious and political rule. The emergence of the institution was not accidental. It was the inevitable outcome of the changes of the class attributes of a part of Buddhist monks after the development of Buddhism. When Buddhism was introduced into Tibet, Tibet was under a regime based on the separation of religion from politics. Thus, first of all, let us have a look into the relationship between politics and religion in various periods of Tibetan history.

According to ancient Tibetan annals, before the introduction of Buddhism into Tibet, during the reigns of twenty-seven *btsan-po* (kings) in succession from Gnya'-khri btsan-po to Lha tho-tho-ri gnyan-btsan, the Tufan regime was under the patronage of the three Tibetan indigenous religions—*Sgrung, Lde'u,* and *Bon.* This gives the reader the mistaken impression that the Tufan regime prior to the introduction of Buddhism was already connected with the Bon religion and was a merger of clerical and secular rule. A careful analysis of the records shows, however, that although there was at the time a spiritual master called *Sku-bon* serving in the *btsan-po*'s palace, he was engaged only in praying for the *btsan-po*'s benefit and held no political power. As recorded in many annals, Gnya'-khri btsan-po, the first *btsan-po* of Tufan, ascended the throne in the Wood Rat year 731 years before the birth of Srong-btsan Sgam-po, i.e., in the Wood Rat year 429 years after the *parinirvana* of the Lord Buddha Sakyamuni.* It was therefore A.D. 115, long before the initiation of the Tibetan way of numbering the years.** During his reign, a man by the name of Tshe-mi gshen-gyi rmu-rgyal reformed Bon, and it became the aboriginal Bon in Tibet. (See *History of Bon-po, Records of Tibetan Kings and Ministers*, written by the Fifth Dalai Lama, and *New Red Annals—A Divine Key to the Royal Lineage* written by Pan-chen Bsod-nams Grags-pa, p. 1625.)

The Bon which spread in Tibet before Gnya'-khri btsan-po was called *Brdol-bon*. It stemmed from primitive religious concepts and it was said to worship indigenous deities in charge of locality, war, household, or maternal family. The Bonists held live sacrifice by killing cows, sheep, deer, and other animals. They believed in previous existence and afterlife, i.e., human beings after death would become spirits, and the spirits might be reborn as human beings. In historical records, this religion was called *Bon-dkar-po* (literally "white Bon religion"). But I

---

*According to Kha-che-pan-chen Shakya-shiri's calculation, the *parinirvana* (literally "complete stillness") of Sakyamuni occurred in 544 B.C. Generally speaking, in India there are two ways of calculating the *parinirvana* of Sakyamuni, in the Han (Chinese) areas there are three ways; and in Tibet there are more than twenty ways. Most Indian Buddhists and foreign historians have adopted Kha-che-pan-chen Shakya-shiri's method of calculation, which is also used in this book.

**The Tibetan way of numbering the years is quite similar to that of the lunar calendar of the Han people. Five elements—iron, wood, water, fire, and earth—are joined to twelve animals—rat, ox, tiger, hare, dragon, serpent, horse, sheep, monkey, cock, dog, and pig. The result is a cycle ending at the sixtieth year. The first cycle of the Tibetan calendar commenced in A.D. 1027, but the year names are also used to describe earlier events. The year 1986 was at the end of the sixteenth cycle.—*Tr.*

2

haven't found any book especially describing its doctrines. During the reign of the eighth *btsan-po* Gri-gum btsan-po, a man named Gshen-rab-mi-bo-che (also called "Gshen-rab, the forefather of Bon") mixed the aboriginal Bon with doctrines of heretical teachers, which were introduced into Tibet through Stag-gzig (the name of Persia in Tibetan). As a mixture of the two, a new religious order was founded, called *'Khyar-bon*, differing from Brdol-bon.

The new Bon was also called *Snang-gshen*. It had no belief in previous existence or afterlife, but held a belief in deities and demons. It was believed that deities were protectors of people, but that demons took away people's spirit after their death and even caused damage to their family and descendants; therefore deities had to be worshipped to ward off demons.

The only books of Bon history I have read are works written by Tibetan Buddhist scholars or found in caves. (In the periods of rivalries among various religious orders, those defeated hid their books in caves or under the earth.) I haven't found any book of Bon history written by Bon scholars. According to the *Biography of Mkha'-'gro yes-shes mtsho-rgyal* (old edition of block printing, Lhasa), under Bon religion four seasonal rites of sacrifice were held: in autumn one thousand deer were killed at one time; in winter the victims were three thousand male yaks, sheep, and goats respectively, and one thousand females respectively, and they were vivisected; in spring the rite of "vivisecting female deer without antlers" was held, during which four does were vivisected after their hoofs were cut off; in summer the rite of "sacrifices offered to the founder of Bon" was held, during which sacrifices were offered along with the burning of trees and crops. When a man was ill, a rite of "offering donations to redeem his life" was held. The number of animals offered for live sacrifice varied from three thousand male and three thousand female animals to no fewer than one male and one female, depending on one's wealth. For

3

the dead, in order to subdue their ghosts, rites of live sacrifice were held as well. Besides, there were rites for other occasions, such as praying for the blessings of the deities, making request for oracles, practising divination, and so on. But the fact that every year such a large number of livestock were killed and used as sacrificial offerings doubtlessly caused great damage to animal husbandry in Tufan, until Srong-btsan Sgam-po ordered a ban on Bon. All this shows us that the Bon religion called Snang-gshen or 'Khyar-bon was a primitive and ethnic religion of Tufan.

2. The Economic and Political Situation in Tibet When Buddhism Was Newly Introduced

The period between Srong-btsan Sgam-po's ascending the throne in the Earth Ox year 1,173 years after the *parinirvana* of the Lord Buddha Sakyamuni (A.D. 629), and Glang-dar-ma's persecution of Buddhism in the Iron Cock year 1,385 years after the *parinirvana* of Sakyamuni (A.D. 841)—a space of 212 years —was considered by Buddhists as the time of the first diffusion of Buddhism in Tibet. This calculation accords with the view that Srong-btsan Sgam-po died at the age of thirty-four. It is based on a comparative study of the following historical events. In the closing years of the reign of Gnam-ri Srung-btsan, Srong-btsan Sgam-po's father, the relationship between Tufan and the Tang court began to be set up. After his accession to the throne, Srong-btsan Sgam-po married Tang princess Wen Cheng. In the seventh year of Khri-ral-pa-can's reign (A.D. 821), a Tang-Tufan peace conference was held. Two years later, Tang-Tufan Peace Pledge Monuments were erected in front of the Jokhang Temple in Lhasa; in Chang'an, the Tang capital city; and on the boundary between Tang and Tufan. After a comparative study of the events mentioned above, I think such a classification of time is preferable.

It was due to the economic and political conditions of interior China and Tibet that Buddhism began its first diffusion in the reign of Srong-btsan Sgam-po. Otherwise it would have been impossible for Buddhism to develop in Tibet. By that time in the hinterland of our country the Tang Dynasty had been founded and had become powerful and prosperous.

In the Earth Tiger year before the initiation of the Tibetan way of numbering years, 1,162 years after the *parinirvana* of Sakyamuni (A.D. 618), when the peasant uprising led by Dou Jiande broke out in Henan and the Sui Dynasty was crumbling, Li Yuan, a high-ranking official at Taiyuan, Shanxi, joined the peasant uprising and led a military expedition against the Sui court. After seizing the capital city of Chang'an, he captured the fruits of the victory of the peasant uprising, ascended the throne, and founded the Tang Dynasty. During the reign of his son Li Shiming (Tai Zong), the political and military strength and well-developed economy and culture of the Tang Dynasty were in full swing, and China then became one of the most powerful and prosperous countries in the world. In the Wood Horse year seventeen years after the founding of the Tang Dynasty, or 1,178 years after the *parinirvana* of Sakyamuni (A.D. 634), Tibetan king Gnam-ri Srung-btsan (Srong-btsan Sgam-po's father) established the first ties with the Tang court. After that, medicine, calendarial calculation, advanced skills and techniques of agriculture and handicraft, etc., were introduced from the hinterland of our country into Tibet, resulting in an unprecedented development of Tibetan society in politics, economy, and culture.

But almost at the same time, there were large-scale revolts of slaves and commoners. According to the Tibetan annals found in Dunhuang (see Bibliography 43), "During the reign of *btsan-po* Srong-btsan Sgam-po, his royal father's ministers and subjects nursed a grievance against him, his queen-mother's ministers and subjects betrayed him, and relatives on his mother's side, such as Zhang-zhung, Sum-po, Dwags-po, Kong-po, and Nyang-po, incited the people to rise in rebellion. His royal father Gnam-ri Srung-btsan was poisoned to death." This shows that in Gtsang, Mnga'-ris, North Gtsang, Nyi, Dwags-po, Kong-po, Nyang-po, and other places large-scale revolts occurred; the slave uprisings dealt heavy blows to the slave-owning system of Tibet and gave impetus to the development of new social production relations.

Up to that time, Tibet had been divided into many small areas by separatist regimes of clans or tribes. Then the people gradually came to realize that this scattered state of affairs not only presented obstacles to unity among tribes, but also hampered the development of social production; they wanted to establish a regime that would unite all the clans and tribes. It was due to the Tibetan people's willingness and desire that Srong-btsan Sgam-po was able to annex the tribal groups and bring them under a central regime, the first centralized political power in Tibet. This was also the first phase of amalgamation of clans and tribes in Tibet in the process of forming a nationality. At that time, Tibetan society was basically a slave-owning system with early feudal economic relations. Some of the Buddhist doctrines accorded with the economic relations of the slave society, while other Buddhist ideas accorded with the economic relations of the feudal society. Buddhism could originate, exist, and develop only in a society which was suitable for the development of these ideas.

Buddhism was introduced into Tibet during the reign of Srong-btsan Sgam-po. Its development was not brought about by its own strength. It was the outcome of the politico-economic development of Tibetan society, and it met the needs of the ruling class for a new religion. If one understands the class character of the laws laid down by Srong-btsan Sgam-po and the nature of property ownership in Tibetan society, one will understand that Tibet already possessed all the objective social conditions necessary for the introduction of Buddhism.

By order of Srong-btsan Sgam-po, the first script for the Tibetan language was created by a sutra translator, Thon-mi-bsam-bho-ta. Twenty-one Buddhist scriptures were translated into Tibetan (the titles can be found in *A Feast for Wise Men*, p. 172), and the Buddhist main doctrines, the "Ten Precepts,"* were embodied in the Tibetan law code. Srong-btsan Sgam-po's reign was also credited with the completion of the first Tibetan legal code, the "Code of Six Laws," which consisted of thirty-six regulations concerning civil and military administration, and administrative division of areas. It made sharp distinctions of social classes according to ranks and behaviours. It stipulated severe penalties for committing murder, theft, and robbery, and special penalties for commoners violating the law. According to the code, all offenders must be punished in accordance with their rank and status. If a high-ranking official offended against the law, he would be judged in consideration of his status. The low-ranking ones would be judged in consideration of their feelings. Here the class distinction was very clear. What deserves mention are the "Six Edicts" in the law code, which clearly stipulated that the subjects should undertake to support their king, be taxed by him, and be loyal to him; servants should be obedient to their masters; noble women should not interfere with political affairs; slaves should not become commoners or soldiers; and women should not attend tribal conferences. The so-called "Fifteen State Laws" stipulated that servants must not flee from their masters, slaves must not be appointed as offi-

---

*The "Ten Precepts" are as follows: (1) kill no living being; (2) abstain from theft and robbery; (3) abstain from debauchery; (4) abstain from telling lies; (5) drink no wine; (6) eat no flesh; (7) do not take part in singing and dancing in musical or theatrical performances nor go to look on or listen; (8) do not adorn thyself with wreaths of fragrant flowers nor anoint thy body with perfume; (9) do not sit on a high, broad, and large couch; (10) refrain from acquiring or possessing uncoined or coined gold, silver, or jewels.—*Tr.*

cials, and so on. In the so-called "Sixteen Laws on Human Relationship," it was stipulated that high-ranking people and elders should be respected and that women's opinions about social or domestic affairs should not be accepted. From all these bans, it can be seen that the authority of king, husband, and clan were at that time established by law.

Obviously, feudal elements were already in existence in the social relations of the Tibetan society. For instance, the "Six Edicts" worked out by Srong-btsan Sgam-po made it a rule that one should keep one's horses off the fields that belonged to the commoners; the wooden slips and official documents in the ancient Tibetan language found in Xinjiang indicate that the peasants were allowed to buy or sell land, that they had to pay taxes after the autumn harvest, and that a system of measure in homestead allotment was established. All these mean that the commoners cultivated with their own tools on their private land —a mode of production that could exist only in a feudal society, not in a slave society. As recorded in ancient Tibetan manuscripts found in the Dunhuang Caves, during the reign of Srong-btsan Sgam-po in succession to Gnam-ri Srung-btsan, Minister Myang-mang-po-rje zhang-snang subjugated the area of Sum-po and levied taxes on the inhabitants there, not through military expedition, but by his wisdom. One of the manuscripts says, "Later, Srong-btsan Sgam-po went to the north on a tour of inspection and also not by military forces succeeded in levying taxes on the Turks and *A-zhas* who were then the subjects of the Tang Dynasty." Since the authorities of government, of divinity, of clan, and of husband marked the Chinese feudal society, the taxation of his subjects by King Srong-btsan Sgam-po indicated the beginning of the Tibetan feudal society, for a king who levied taxes was rather a landlord than a slave owner. On this subject, my opinion is similar to that of many scholars: that in the days of Srong-btsan Sgam-po the Tibetan society was based basically on slavery, but that some feudal economic elements had already appeared in it. In that period of Tibetan social development, the Bon religion began to lose its control over the thoughts of the people. In its stead Buddhism, which conformed with the new social-economic relationship, arose to meet the needs of the ruling class.

We must not explain the process of social development with superstitious ideas; on the contrary, we should explain the superstitious ideas with historical facts. First, we should explore the objective contents of a certain process of social development in a specific time and under specific conditions, then make out which class was the main motive power that boosted the progressive development of society.

The founder of Buddhism was Sakyamuni. (*The General History of China* published recently in the Han language says that Sakyamuni was born in 556 B.C., died in 475 B.C., and was six years older than Confucius.) The Buddhism he founded was a reflection of his view of Indian socio-economic relations at the time, and a world outlook emerged in the process. This world outlook, assuming the form of Buddhism, in turn exercised great influence on the people's minds. The Buddhist order was a superstructure of ideas which reflected the objective social existence and the economic base. For instance, Buddhism held that the highest caste consisted of persons from royal families; the second highest caste consisted of nobles; and the lowest caste, Sudra, consisted of blacksmiths, butchers, fishermen, and so forth. This shows that Buddhism attached great importance to the authority of clans. Besides, it stressed that slaves should not oppose the slave owners, but should obey them; to obey their masters and endure hardships are slaves' best merits; slaves should not be admitted to monkhood without the permission of their masters. It also propagated that women should obey their husbands and serve them as slaves served their masters, and this was considered by Buddhism as one of women's "eight merits." This clearly shows that it attached great importance to the authority of the husband. All these were marks of the economic relationship of a slave society and a feudal society. It was because Buddhism conformed with the socio-economic relationship of the then Tibetan society that it enjoyed the patronage of Srong-btsan Sgam-po and spread into Tibet.

Srong-btsan Sgam-po had the Buddhist doctrines embodied in laws and made it a rule that the Tufan people must adhere to Buddhism. This indicates that Buddhism began to have an influence on politics, and that Buddhism was used to consolidate the *btsan-po*'s rule. At that time in Tibet there were no professional Buddhist monks or temples for monks to live in. The monks had no special status or privileges. Srong-btsan Sgam-po was only a *btsan-po*, not a hierarch of a religious order. So it is quite evident that Tibetan polity based on the merging of religious and secular rule had not yet been established.

Later, in the Wood Monkey year before the initiation of the Tibetan way of numbering years, 1,249 years after the *parinirvana* of the Lord Buddha (A.D. 705), *btsan-po* Khri-lde-gtsug-btsan ascended the throne. He sent two ministers, Bran-ka Mu-le-ko-sha and Gnyags Dznya-na-ku-ma-ra, on a pilgrimage for Buddhist scriptures to India. In the Gangdis Mountains they met two Indian panditas, Sangs-rgyas-gsang-ba and Sangs-rgyas-zhi-ba, who were engaged in Buddhist cultivation and meditation there. From them the two Tufan ministers learnt by heart such Buddhist scriptures as *Agama Sutra*, *S'uvarna Prabhasa, Yoga Tantra*, and *Spyod-rgyud*. Then they returned and offered the memorized scriptures to the *btsan-po*. In order to store the scriptures in a proper place, the *btsan-po* built five temples: Lha-sa-kha-brag, Brag-mar-mgrin-bzang, Brag-mar-ge-ru, Mchims-phu-na-ra, and Ma-sa-gong.

In the Wood Horse year before the initiation of the Tibetan way of numbering years, 1,298 years after the *parinirvana* of the Lord Buddha (A.D. 754), *btsan-po* Khri-lde-gtsug-btsan sent a four-member group on a pilgrimage for Buddhist scriptures to Emperor Xuan Zong of the Tang Dynasty. The group was led by Sangs-shi, son of Ba-de-wu, an ex-official of the Tang court who was alleged to have come into Tibet accompanying Princess Jin Cheng. The emperor bestowed on them a thousand volumes of scriptures written in gold on blue paper. Then they paid a visit to monk Nyi-ma, who lived in the vicinity of Wutai in Shanxi, to make a request for Buddhist scriptures. The monk gave them three scriptures—*Dge-ba-bcu, Vadjra Tchtchhedika Pradjnaparamita*, and *S'alisambhava Sutra*—and said that if they would offer the three scriptures to the *btsan-po* in that sequence, the *btsam-po* would adhere to Buddhism. However, while Sangs-shi was still on his way back to Tibet with all these scriptures, *btsan-po* Khri-lde-gtsug-btsan fell from his horse and died at Rgya-ma-khri-khang.*

3. Rivalries Between Buddhism and Bon

Records of the first rivalry between Buddhism and Bon can be found only in two ancient Tibetan annals. *Byams-ma*, a text on Bon history, said that Srong-btsan Sgam-po lived only thirty-five years because of his hatred for Bon, while *The Biography of Mkha'-'gro-yes-shes rgya-mtsho* said that Srong-btsan Sgam-po proscribed Bon because of its large-scale live sacrifices. This shows that the struggle between Buddhism and Bon had already occurred by that time. To our knowledge there are no other historical records about this incident.

The second rivalry occurred during the reign of Khri-srong-lde-btsan, who ascended the throne in the Fire Monkey year (A.D. 756) in succession to Khri-lde-gtsug-btsan at the age of

---

*This version of the incident appears in *The Records of the Bsam-yas Monastery, Religious History of Yar-lung*, and *Religious History of Lho-brag*. But according to the inscriptions on the stone monument erected in front of the Potala Palace at Lhasa, *btsan-po* Khri-lde-gtsug-btsan was murdered by his ministers 'Bal-stong-tshab and Glang-me-gzig.

sixteen. He reigned for twenty-five years. In the first period of his reign, because he was too young, all the ruling power was taken over by Minister Ma-zhang Grom-pa-skyes, who had also been the minister of Khri-lde-gtsug-btsan, Khri-srong-lde-btsan's father. Ma-zhang Grom-pa-skyes professed the Bon religion and opposed Buddhism. He proclaimed that the Buddhist doctrines on rebirth were baseless; the only way to escape the evils of demons was to profess Bon; those who engaged in Buddhist ceremonies would be divested of properties and exiled to remote areas. Tufans were permitted to profess the Bon religion only. Sacrifices could not be offered to the dead with Buddhist ceremony; all the Buddhist images in the Ramoche Temple that came from the Han area were to be sent back. He ordered that Lha-sa-kha-brag Temple and Brag-mar-mgrin-bzang Temple in Lhasa be destroyed. As the Unmovable Vadjra statue in the Ramoche Temple was too heavy to be moved away even by three hundred men, it was buried in a sandbank nearby. Then by his orders, two statues of Sakyamuni in the Jokhang Temple and the Ramoche Temple were sent to Skyid-grong in the Mnga'-ris region; all the Han monks in Lhasa were sent back to the hinterland; the Jokhang Temple and the Ramoche Temple were transformed into workshops and slaughterhouses; the Buddhist statues there were covered with the skins and intestines of killed animals. Two ministers, Lang-me-gzig and 'Bal-stong-tshab, were condemned to death for adhering to Buddhism.*

---

*According to Sba-bzhed (Records of the Bsam-yas Monastery), they were killed because they adhered to Buddhism. But according to the stone tablet "The Memorial to Stag-sgra klu-khong" erected in front of Potala Palace, they were condemned to death because they murdered Khri-lde-gtsug-btsan, and while they were plotting to murder Khri-srong-lde-btsan, their scheme was discovered by Minister Stag-sgra klu-khong. The enlarged edition of Sba-bzhed says that Minister Stag-sgra klu-khong was in favour of Bon and against Buddhism and was opposed to the building of the Bsam-yas Monastery; as a result he was arrested and exiled to North Gtsang.

Just at the time when Ma-zhang Grom-pa-skyes was vigorously persecuting Buddhism, Sangs-shi returned from the hinterland to Lhasa, and he was compelled to hide the scriptures brought from the hinterland in caves at Mchims-phu in the Bsam-yas area. Buddhist minister Gsal-snang fled to Mon-yul in the Mnga'-ris region. When *btsan-po* Khri-srong-lde-btsan grew up and took over the political administrative power, he ordered Minister Sangs-shi to translate the Buddhist scriptures he had brought back from interior China into Tibetan. So Sangs-shi together with Me-mgo, a Han translator, and Kha-che-a-nan-da, a Tibetan translator, began to do the work secretly. But ministers Ma-zhang and Stag-sgra klu-khong found them out and warned them that if they did not stop, they would be as severely punished as those Buddhists who had been condemned to exile. The translators were so frightened that they had to stop their work and hide the scriptures again in the caves.

Later, the *btsan-po* sent Minister Sangs-shi to Mon-yul in the Mnga'-ris region to help Gsal-snang and consulted secretly with other Buddhist ministers on the question of spreading Buddhism in Tibet. They all agreed that to do this, they must first of all get rid of the influential Minister Ma-zhang, and they decided to kill him.

Not long after their meeting, the Buddhist ministers 'Gos-khri-bzang and Zhang-nya-bzang gave bribes to the *btsan-po*'s messengers, fortune-tellers, and magicians and made them declare that a catastrophe would happen to the Tufan regime that year, which could be escaped only by having an influential minister kept alive in a tomb for a few days. Their words spread far and wide and were known to all and even to Ma-zhang himself. Then 'Gos-khri-bzang called a conference of ministers at which he made an impassioned speech. He declared that in order to free the *btsan-po* and the government from the catastrophe, the most influential Tufan minister should be kept alive in a tomb for a few days, and it was he who should be the one because he was the most influential minister. Not to be outdone, Ma-zhang proudly declared that *he* was the most influential minister and should be chosen for the honor. The result was that 'Gos-khri-bzang and Ma-zhang went together into a tomb at Stod-lung. When the entrance of the tomb was about to be closed, 'Gos-khri-bzang put on disguise and escaped from the tomb. But Ma-zhang was buried alive. That was the end of the second rivalry between Bon and Buddhism.

Then followed the third rivalry between the two religions. In order to spread Buddhism, Khri-srong-lde-btsan invited Bo-dhi-swa-to,* who was then in Nepal, to come to preach Buddhist doctrines such as the "Ten Moral Commandments" and "Twelve Chains of Causation"** at Lung-tshub pho-brang in Bsam-yas. Two months later, disasters happened one after another. The 'Phang-thang pho-brang at Bsam-yas was destroyed by flood. Thunderstorms damaged the palace standing on Dmar-po-ri Hill at Lhasa. People and their animals suffered from epidemic diseases. Rainstorms and drought struck the crops. The local people considered that all these disasters were caused by the diffusion of Buddhism in Tibet. They asked the *btsan-po* to send the Indian monk back to Nepal, which, in face of the strong anti-Buddhist sentiment, *btsan-po* Khri-srong-lde-btsan agreed to do. On leaving, Bo-dhi-swa-to proposed that the Tufan *btsan-po* invite pandita Padmasambhava*** in case he himself was ever

---

*A prince of Bangladesh. He and Atisha belonged to the same clan.

**The "Twelve Chains of Causation" or "Twelve Causes of Existence," the fundamental dogma of Buddhist thought, are the concatenation of cause and effect in the whole range of existence through twelve links, the understanding of which solves the riddle of life, revealing the inanity of existence and preparing the mind for Nirvana. They are: *Djaramarana* (decrepitude and death), *Djati* (birth), *Bhava* (existence), *Upadana* (grasp), *Trichna* (love), *Vedana* (sensation), *Spars's* (contact), *Chadayatana* (the organs of sensation), *Namarupa* (name and form), *Vidjnana* (knowledge), *Samskara* (action), and *Avidya* (absence of perception, viz. ignorance which mistakes the illusory phenomena of this world for realities).—*Tr.*

***Padmasambhava was the son of the king of O-rgyan, now Afghanistan.

invited to Tibet for the second time.

The *btsan-po* held consultation again with his Buddhist ministers and, in order to make the people realize that Buddhism was more reliable than Bon, sent a thirty-man group including ministers Gsal-snang and Sangs-shi with a lot of presents to pay a respectful visit to Emperor Su Zong of the Tang Dynasty on a pilgrimage for Buddhist scriptures. The Tang emperor honoured the Tufan *btsan-po* by giving him many scriptures written with gold on blue paper together with a hat made of gold and silver, ten thousand bolts of silk and satin, and a big coloured wooden plate. The bestowals for the Minister Gsal-snang included one hundred ounces of gold leaves, with a decoration of birds on each, five hundred bolts of silk and satin, a vase made of gold and silver, a plate made of one hundred ounces of gold, and ten strings of pearl rosaries. There were gifts for all the others as well. After returning to Lhasa, they offered the *btsan-po* Khri-srong-lde-btsan the box containing the imperial edict and the bestowals, including the Buddhist scriptures. Then the *btsan-po* sent Minister Gsal-snang to Nepal to invite Bo-dhi-swa-to to Tibet for the second time. Bo-dhi-swa-to in turn invited Pandita Padmasambhava to go with him. They met at Mon-yul in the Mnga'-ris region, then made a trip by boat to Dbu-ru in the Shangs region. When they came to Bsam-yas, Bo-dhi-swa-to preached Buddhist teachings, and Padmasambhava showed off various kinds of magic power. He introduced a kind of divination in which spirits were called to descend on children whose parents were still alive, and thus initiated into Tibet the rite of sacrifice known as "calling the spirits." Later, when the Buddhists were planning to build the Bsam-yas Monastery, not only the Bonist ministers such as Stag-sgra klu-khong, but also the *btsan-po*'s wife Cog-ro-bza' stood up to oppose it. They proclaimed that Buddhism was not superior to Bon in power, and it was no good to profess Buddhism. On the other hand, the Buddhist ministers, the

15

monks from Han territories, and Indian panditas stated that Buddhism and Bon, like fire and water, could not coexist; the coexistence of the two in the same place would be an evil omen. They proposed that in order to prove which of the two religions was more reliable, a contest or debate between them should be held; should the Bonists gain the upper hand, the Buddhists monks would go back to their homeland willingly; but should the Buddhists win the debate, the Bon religion would be abolished in Tibet and Buddhism would be preached there. The *btsan-po* approved of their proposal. So in the Earth Pig year before the initiation of the Tibetan way of numbering year, 1,303 years after the *parinirvana* of the Lord Buddha (A.D. 759), a debate between Bonists and Buddhists was held in front of a palace at Zur-phu in Mal-gro. The debate ended with the failure of the Bonists. As a result, the Bon priests were exiled to Mnga'ris and Zhang-zhung, and the Bon scriptures were collected to be thrown into waters or buried under a black pagoda in the Bsam-yas Monastery. Bon ceremonies, such as blood sacrifices and prayers for the living and the dead, were put under ban. The Tufans were allowed to profess Buddhism only, and Bon was prohibited.

While proscribing Bon, Khri-srong-lde-btsan retained some Bon ceremonies such as "praying for blessings," "doing away with evils," "cremation" and "making pledges around a bonfire." The Buddhists made use of their forms, but changed their contents. On the other hand, *Bsgyur-bon*—the Bon religion which arose after the fall of the Tufan regime—remoulded the doctrines of Buddhism into that of Bon and thus transformed itself into a new Bon with newly created theories. This shows that the rivalries between Bon and Buddhism brought changes to both. To adapt itself to the circumstances, each tried to absorb something from the other, i.e., to remould its own contents while retaining its forms. This represented a new development of both Bon and Buddhism. For this reason, some modern historians call the Tibetan Buddhism "Lamaism," but this does not accord with the hard facts, because they look only at the surface of things and do not consider the objective reality.

4. The Earliest Tibetan Buddhist Monks and the Formation of the Rnying-ma Sect*

The construction of the Bsam-yas Monastery began in the Water Tiger year before the initiation of the Tibetan way of numbering years, 1,306 years after the *parinirvana* of the Buddha (A.D. 762), and was completed four years later. In the year after its completion, the Fire Sheep year (A.D. 767), in order to make sure whether Tibetans could become professional monks or not, the *btsan-po* invited twelve *bhikchu* monks of Sarvasti-vadah (the school which discusses the existence of everything) to Tibet from India. Bo-dhi-swa-to acted as the *mkhan-po* (the chief instructor of the novices). With twelve *bhikchu* monks as his assistants, he held a tonsure ceremony for seven Tibetans and admitted them into the priesthood. They were Rba-gsal-snang, Sang-shi, Rma-rin-chen-mshog, 'Khon Klu'i-dbang-po-srung, Pa-gor Bee-ro-tsa-na, Ngan-lam Rgyal-ba-mchog-dbyang, and La-gsum rgyal-ba'i byang-chub. These seven people were the first Tibetan monks, and they were called the "seven novices."

Then the *btsan-po* ordered the Buddhists among Tufan ministers, princesses, and commoners to join the priesthood. But they refused, saying that to become monks or nuns would make them unable to make their living, or to pay taxes and do civil and military service for the *btsan-po*, which would be regarded as a violation of the law. So the *btsan-po* prescribed

---

Rnying-ma means "ancient" or "old." This Buddhist sect preaches old Tantras. It attaches great importance to esoteric rather than exoteric doctrines. Its monks are allowed to get married and take part in productive labour. They wear red hats and therefore are called the Red Hat Sect.

that monks would be exempted from taxation, military obliga-
tion, and compulsory labour and would receive donations from
the *btsan-po*'s treasury for their living. From this we can clearly
see two aspects of life at that time. One is that Tibetan Buddhist
monks led a parasitic life. The other is that all subjects, except
monks, of the *btsan-po* were liable for taxation, military service,
and labour obligations. Due to the *btsan-po*'s encouragement,
the number of monks in Tibet grew to 305 in a year. All these
monks were later ordained as *atcharya* (teachers of morals) who
preached Buddhist doctrines. Among them, the *mkhan-po* (abbot) enjoyed the highest authority. The first *mkhan-po* was
Bo-dhi-swa-to.* He and *atcharya* Padmasambhava were religious
leaders only and had no political privileges, not even the right
to attend administrative conferences. They could only make
reports to the *btsan-po* in case they had a problem. But the
btsan-po could not make any decisions on important problems
by himself; such decisions could only be made at the *'don-sa.***
If the *'don-sa* was not consulted, any important decisions made
by the *btsan-po* alone was not valid. And the *btsan-po* had to
issue orders according to the decisions made at the *'don-sa* even
if he did not agree with them. This strict rule under which the
btsan-po could not act arbitrarily is recorded in *Sba-bzhed*
("Record of the Bsam-yas Monastery"). The incidents in which
Bo-dhi-swa-to and Padmasambhava were sent back to India and
the discussion of the construction of the Bsam-yas Monastery
were all instances of it.

During the several years when Padmasambhava stayed in
Tufan, he preached many esoteric scriptures to the *btsan-po* and
his ministers. In Tibetan annals the doctrines he preached were
called "ancient esoteric Buddhism," as opposed to the many new

---

*His other name was Zhi-ba-'tsho.

** *'Don-sa* was a consultative conference attended by the Tufan *btsan-po* and
his major and minor ministers. It was probably under the influence of the Tang
court that Srong-btsan Sgam-po inaugurated this institution.

esoteric scriptures translated into Tibetan by Rin-chen bzang-po of the Mnga'-ris region at the end of the 10th century when Buddhism revived in Tibet. Esoteric doctrines preached after that time were called "new esoteric Buddhism."

Before the death of Bo-dhi-swa-to, the Tibetan monks took their daily necessities from the *btsan-po*'s treasury and had no other stable source of income.

5. The Transformation of Some Tibetan Buddhist Monks from Slave Owners into Feudal Landlords Owning Monasterial Estates

The *Records of the Bsam-yas Monastery* written during Khri-srong-lde-btsan's reign has three different editions: enlarged, regular, and abridged. The main points of the *Enlarged Records of the Bsam-yas Monastery*, which was included in the *Religious History of Lho-brag* written by Dpa'-bo gtsug-lay 'phreng-ba, are as follows. After the death of *mkhan-po* Bo-dhi-swa-to, the *btsan-po* appointed Rba Ye-shes-dbang-po* as *mkhan-po* and set up a religious conference of Buddhists, which was superior to the *'don-sa* of ministers; and he granted the *mkhan-po*, the religious hierarch, an honorific title of *gser-yig-pa-chen-po* ("royal envoy with a golden plate") and the privilege of attending the conference of ministers, with his status superior to that of all the ministers. As mentioned above, at that time the monks were provided with supplies from the *btsan-po*'s treasury, but the amount of supplies was not fixed. So the *btsan-po* came to think, if he failed to stipulate the amount of supplies for the Bsam-yas Monastery and for the *mkhan-po* and monks, after his death they would be left without any care or support. Thus he planned to allocate three hundred slave house-

---

*His original name was Rba-gsal-snang. This name was given to him by his Buddhist tutor when he joined the monkhood.

holds to the monastery and seven slave households to each monk, so that the slaves would be responsible for the support of the monastery and monks. When the *btsan-po* told Rba Ye-shes-dbang-po[*] about his idea, the latter said that in view of the fact that the *btsan-po* had bestowed nine hundred households on the minister who had rendered meritorious services, the amount of bestowal for the monastery and monks appeared to him rather proper, but if by any chance the royal family held different views, or if there were any epidemic diseases, famine, or military invasions, the supplies from the allocated households might not be secured, so from a long-term point of view it would be better to allocate two hundred households of slaves to the Bsam-yas Monastery and three households to each monk, the ownership of the slaves being granted to the monks. Thus, the monastery was entitled to own 150 households, and each monk to own three households. As a result, there were 1,065 households or 4,260 persons (a household was supposed to have four members: man and wife, a son, and a daughter) supporting the Bsam-yas Monastery and its 305 monks. These households were exempted from taxes and civil or military services.

As to the *mkhan-po* and the monks' daily necessities, they still came from the taxes paid by the people to the *btsan-po*. Thus the Buddhist hierarch *mkhan-po* was provided annually with nine hundred *khal* of barley (seventy-five *khal* per month), 1,100 taels of yak butter (1 *khal* and $2\frac{1}{2}$ *nya-ga* per month), a suit of monk cloth, a horse, four bundles of paper, three pieces of Chinese ink, and salt which could be provided whenever it was used up. Each of the twenty-five monks (or *sgom-chen*) who devoted themselves to meditation at Mchims-phu in the Bsam-yas area was provided with fifty-five *khal* of barley, eight hundred taels of yak butter, a horse, and six suits of clothes. The thirteen sutra teachers were provided with as much as the

---

[*]The then *mkhan-po*.

sgom-chen. Each of the twenty-five novice monks who were learning scriptures was provided annually with twenty-five *khal* of barley and three suits of clothes. Each of the ordinary monks was provided with eight *khal* of barley and two bundles of paper per year. Although the *mkhan-po* and monks personally did not own any land, pasture, or livestock, the barley they got annually as donations from the royal storehouse numbered as much as 5,428 *khal*, which was equivalent to the amount of consumption of 542 peasants in a year. The *mkhan-po*, meditators, and teachers altogether were only thirty-nine in number, but they received annually 31,500 taels of butter, which was enough to feed 181 peasants for a year, with eighteen head of cattle per peasant. All this shows that the monks at that time, although they constituted a very small portion of the population, received large amounts of supplies from the *btsan-po*, were slave owners, and formed a privileged stratum exempted from taxes and corvée.

Mu-ne *btsan-po* and Khri-lde-srong-btsan Sad-na-legs-mcing-yon* in succession followed Khri-srong-lde-btsan's policy concerning Buddhism.

Btsan-po Khri-ral-pa-can's reign lasted for twenty-two years, beginning in the Wood Sheep year prior to the initiation of the Tibetan way of numbering years, 1,359 years after the *parinirvana* of Sakyamuni (A.D. 815). As a devoted Buddhist, the *btsan-po* raised the monks to the highest social stratum and granted seven households of peasants to each monk. By his order, any one who looked at a monk with an evil eye or pointed at a monk with an evil finger would have his eyes gouged out or his finger cut off. He granted some monasteries land, livestock, and slaves. The inscription on the monument raised by a minister named Zhang-tshe-spong sto-re in front of the Lcang-

---

*According to the inscription on the monument in the Rje-sde-ka-byung Monastery, Khri-lde-srong-btsan and Sad-na-legs-mcing-yon are two names of a person. Khri-lde-srong-btsan was the son of Khri-srong-lde-btsan.

bu Monastery at Stod-lung lcang-bu*, states: "The monastery was built by Khri-gtsug-lde-btsan's order to worship the Three Precious Ones (the Buddha, the law, and the priesthood); it houses four monks and has been granted by the *btsan-po* the adjacent land and pastureland, livestock, ritual instruments, and other things as its stable properties." All the Tibetan historians now consider that Khri-gtsug-lde-btsan was none other than Khri-ral-pa-can. It is obvious that the assignment of estates and pastureland to monasteries began in Khri-ral-pa-can's reign. So, in my view, Buddhist monks prior to that time formed a class of slave owners who possessed slave households, but no estates, pastureland, or livestock. Nevertheless, since Khri-ral-pa-can assigned estates, pastureland, and livestock to monasteries, some of the monks began to become landlords.

6. The Persecution of Buddhism by Glang-dar-ma

The following account is based on the last part of the *Records of the Bsam-yas Monastery*. In the reign of Khri-ral-pa-can, each monk enjoyed patronage by seven households of peasants. Whoever stared at monks with malicious eyes was to have them gouged out, whoever pointed an accusing finger at monks was to have it cut off, whoever scolded monks was to have his tongue cut out, whoever stole monks' belongings or the property of a monastery was to be fined eightyfold. This aroused strong aversion and opposition from ministers and people who opposed Buddhism. They said that they could not regard themselves as free men until these prescriptions were cancelled. So these ministers conspired secretly. They understood that only after they had succeeded in killing *btsan-po* Khri-ral-pa-can, Minister Bran-ka-dpal-yon, and Queen Ngang-tshul-ma could they put Buddhism under ban. And they

---

*Stod-lung lcang-bu is where the Mtshur-phur Monastery now stands.

thought, since Khri-ral-pa-can had no son, if he was killed, the ruling power would fall into the hands of his elder brother Gtsang-ma. Thus they decided to kill Gtsang-ma first, then Minister Bran-ka-dpal-yon and Queen Ngang-tshul-ma, because if these three people were killed, *btsan-po* Khri-ral-pa-can would be isolated and easier to wipe out.

Thus, Minister Sbas-stag-sna bribed magicians and fortune-tellers and got them spreading rumors that unless *btsan-po*'s brother Gtsang-ma was banished, the kingdom would meet with misfortune. Consequently, Gtsang-ma was banished to Chumbi valley, and was poisoned halfway there at 'Khor-lding in the Lho-brag area by Sna-nam mang-mo-rje. Then the ministers lodged a false accusation against Queen Ngang-tshul-ma and Minister Bran-ka-dpal-yon, accusing them of criminal intimacy, and the *btsan-po* ordered that they be executed. Hearing this, the queen committed suicide. But the minister Bran-ka-dapl-yon thought that if he were to be killed, the *btsan-po* would be wiped out by the conspirators. So he escaped to the north of Gtsang and hid himself somewhere underground. At first, the *btsan-po* did not know where he had fled and made a search for him. Then a blind beggar discovered his whereabouts and informed against him. Finally he was executed at Sinye-thang and his body was displayed in public. Later, in the Iron Cock year when Khri-ral-pa-can was thirty-six years of age, he got drunk one day in the Bright-Pure Palace at Mal-gro. His ministers Sbas-stag-sna, Cog-ro-lha-lod, and Legs-sdug-btsan took the opportunity and murdered him.

His brother Glang-dar-ma, who was opposed to Buddhism, was enthroned, and Sbas-stag-sna became the chief minister. While they were whipping up anti-Buddhism opinions, Tufan was hit by epidemic diseases, frost, hailstorms, droughts, and floods, one after another. The anti-Buddhism ministers and people attributed the disasters to the diffusion of Buddhism in Tufan. This happened at a time when science had not been developed and the people could not resist natural disasters, so it was understandable that they attributed these disasters to supernatural powers. They had found that Buddhism could not protect them from such calamities. Even today in some countries highly developed in science and industry, there are many people who sincerely believe in religion, and many others who relate natural disasters to religious belief. In order to secure his ruling position, *btsan-po* Glang-dar-ma took advantage of the people's anti-Buddhism sentiments and skepticism to spread anti-Buddhism opinions and thus succeeded in exterminating Buddhism with rapid and fierce measures. Obviously without the people's anti-Buddhism sentiments, it would have been impossible for Glang-dar-ma to supress Buddhism so thoroughly just by issuing orders.

Glang-dar-ma told the people that the statue of Sakyamuni brought to Tufan by Princess Wen Cheng was that of an Indian devil, which had caused Indian troop failures when it was in India; after it had been brought to Han territories, ominous things happened there; and many misfortunes had occurred since it had been brought to Tufan. He proclaimed that the princess was a female demon who, pretending to make a geographical survey of Tufan, practised geomancy and destroyed the good natural conditions in order to put Tufan under the direct jurisdiction of the Tang Dynasty. Therefore it would be necessary to ban Buddhism, destroy Buddhist temples and monasteries, and compel all monks to leave the religious order.

Thus, Glang-dar-ma proceeded to destroy the Jokhang Temple at Lhasa. He ordered that the two statues of the Buddha be thrown into the river. But officials who were in favour of Buddhism hid the statues of the Buddha under sand and threw rocks into the water instead. The entrances to temples and monasteries were walled up and plastered. Large numbers of Buddhist scriptures were burned or thrown into the water although many of them were hidden by Buddhist believers. The monks were forced to leave the religious order. The high-ranking monks were killed, the middle-level monks were banished to the borderland, the ordinary monks became commoners who had to pay taxes and do labour obligations. Those who refused to do so were sent to hunt wild beasts. So a number of Buddhists fled to Qinghai and Gansu via Mnga'-ris.

Glang-dar-ma, in his turn, was assassinated at the age of forty-four in the Fire Dragon year of the Tibetan calendar (A.D. 846). One day when Glang-dar-ma was reading the inscription on the Tang-Tufan peace pledge monument in front of the Jokhang Temple at Lhasa, a Buddhist named Lha-lung-dpal-gyi-rdo-rje, pretending to make an obeisance to the *btsan-po*, assassinated him with an arrow hidden in his sleeve. The Buddhist then fled to Qinghai, taking with him three sacred sutras: *Anakchara Granthaka Rotchana Garbha Sutra, Karma Sutra*, and *Abhidharma Kocha Karaka' astra*.

The drive against Buddhism continued. It went so far that the influences of Buddhism were completely rooted out in the Dbus, Gtsang, and Mnga'-ris regions. This was called "Persecution of Buddhism" in the Tibetan annals. In spite of this, Esoteric Buddhism continued to be practised secretly by many non-monk people. They tried their best to protect the remains of Buddhist temples, sutras, and statues, which played an important role later when Buddhism revived on an unprecedented scale in the second diffusion of Buddhism. History shows us that forcible prohibition against the religious beliefs of broad masses of people, and attempts to exterminate a religion through political and legal measures, can lead only to contrary results.

7. Period of Chaos in Tufan and Interior China

In the closing years of the Tang Dynasty, the internal struggle for power among the ruling class was intensified. In the

Wood Sheep year before the initiation of the Tibetan way of numbering years, 1,299 years after the *parinirvana* of Sakyamuni (A.D. 755), the Tang generals An Lushan and Shi Siming launched an insurrection against the Tang court. The war lasted eight years and caused great damage to the economy of the northern part of our country. After that, the Tang court began to decline in political power, military strength, and economy. In the Earth Hare year before the initiation of the Tibetan way of numbering years, 1,403 years after the *parinirvana* of Sakyamuni (A.D. 859), Wang Xianzhi precipitated a rebellion. Shortly after that, uprisings of peasants broke out in many places one after another. This period was marked by endless wars between the Tang central government and local separatist regimes and by struggles for power among the Tang officials. The territory under the domination of the central government became smaller and smaller. After the Iron Dragon year prior to the initiation of the Tibetan way of numbering years, 1,404 years after the *parinirvana* of Sakyamuni (A.D. 860), the relationship between the Tang central government and the Tufan regime was broken up. In the Fire Hare year prior to the initiation of the Tibetan way of numbering years, 1,451 years after the *parinirvana* of Sakyamuni (A.D. 907), the Tang Dynasty collapsed.

During the following seventy-two years, the hinterland of our country split into Five Dynasties and Ten Kingdoms successively. The Five Dynasties were (1) the Later Liang Dynasty with Kaifeng in Henan Province as its capital city, three reigns; (2) the Later Tang Dynasty with Loyang in Henan Province as its capital city, four reigns; (3) the Later Jin Dynasty with Kaifeng in Henan as its capital city, two reigns; (4) the Later Han Dynasty with Kaifeng in Henan as its capital city, two reigns; and (5) the Later Zhou Dynasty with Kaifeng in Henan as its capital city, three reigns. The Ten Kingdoms were (1) the Former Shu with Chengdu in Sichuan Province as its capital city, two reigns; (2) Jingnan with Jiangling in Hubei Province as its capital city, five reigns; (3) the Later Shu with Chengdu in Sichuan as its capital city, two reigns; (4) the Southern Han with Guangzhou in Guangdong Province as its capital city, four reigns; (5) the Southern Tang with modern Nanjing in Jiangsu Province as its capital city, three reigns; (6) the Wu with Yangzhou in Jiangsu Province as its capital city, four reigns; (7) the Chu with Changsha in Hunan Province as its capital city, six reigns; (8) the Min with Fuzhou in Fujian Province as its capital city, five reigns; (9) the Wuyue with Hangzhou in Zhejiang Province as its capital city, five reigns; and (10) the Northern Han with Taiyuan in Shanxi Province as its capital city, four reigns. The so-called Five Dynasties and Ten Kingdoms in history were not independent states separated from China, but separatist local regimes within China.

In the period of more than sixty years from the decline of the Tang Dynasty to the Tang-Tufan peace pledge, there were continuous wars between Tang and Tufan on their borders; each had its gains and losses. During the reign of Khri-srong-lde-btsan, the Tufan troops captured many Tang strongholds, even its capital city Chang'an, with the result that the Tang Emperor Dai Zong fled from Chang'an and a new emperor was put on the throne by the Tufan *btsan-po*. During this period the political and military power of the Tufan *btsan-po* reached its height. In the Iron Ox year of Khri-ral-pa-can's reign (A.D. 821), a Tang-Tufan peace pledge was arranged. During the following two years, Tang-Tufan peace pledge monuments were erected in the capital cities of both sides and on their borders. But in the Iron Dragon year, 1,404 years after the *parinirvana* of our Sakyamuni, the Tang-Tufan relationship was broken up. In Tufan, the ruling power of the descendants of Gnya'-khri btsan-po began to decline. In the second year after the assassination of Glang-dar-ma, his two sons, princes 'Od-srung (his concubine's son) and Yum-brtan (his queen's son) were born. Thus there was a great dispute between the queen and the concubine about the princes' rightful succession to the throne, which led to hostility between the two women. Each of the princes had his own supporters. The nobles who backed 'Od-srung became entrenched in Giyo-ru, and the nobles who backed Yum-brtan were entrenched in Dbu-ru. They divided into two factions called "major and minor," "majority and minority," "gold branch and jade leaf," or "meat-eaters and barley-eaters." The rivalry led to a war which lasted twenty-eight years. In the Earth Ox year prior to the initiation of the Tibetan way of numbering years, 1,413 years after the *pari-nirvana* of Sakyamuni (A.D. 869), the largest peasant rebellions in Tufan history broke out throughout the district of Tufan. The first uprising was led by Dbas Kho-gzher-legs-stong in Mdo-khams (Chab-mdo, Xikang, and A-mdo). Then the war between the Bro family and the Sbas family in the Dbu-ru region resulted in an uprising led by Dbas Lo-pho-lo-chung. Another insurrectionary force led by Mchim Kong-mi-drug and Shud-pu Stag-rtse-gnyags arose in Lho-kha, Dwags-po, Kong-po, and other regions. These were the largest rebellions of slaves and commoners in Tufan history. They dealt a heavy blow to the power of slave owners and landlords. They not only put an end to the epoch in which Tufan was ruled by the descend-ants of Gnya'-khri btsan-po and Srong-btsan Sgam-po, but also caused the system of Buddhist teachings and monks in cassocks to disappear in a space of 137 years.[*]

This storm of revolts by slaves and commoners led to Tibet's being split into eleven separatist local regimes: (1) one led by the 'Bro and Cog-ro families in the Gtsang-stod (Gtsang mnga'-ris) region, with Grom-pa-lha-rtse as its capital town; (2) one led by the Myang and Snang families in the Gzhu-snye-mo region, with 'Brang-mkhar-bye-btsan as its capital town; (3) one led by the Sgro and Rma families in the 'Phan-po region, with

---

[*]Calculated on the assumption that Srong-btsan Sgam-po lived thirty-five years.

Za-damn as its capital town; (4) one led by the Mchim and Gnya' families, in the Yar-lung-stod region, with Sna-mo-yar-rtse and Mar-rtse as its capital towns; (5) one led by the Sny-ba and Zhur-bu families in the Lho-brag-gtam-shul region, with Bya-tshang-gung-snang as its capital town; and (6) one led by the Khu and Gnyags families in the 'Phyong-rgyas region, with Khu-gud-co-mkhar as its capital town. In addition, there were local regimes at Dol-po, Kong-po, Gnyal, and Lhasa. Thus, Tufan was all split up until the Earth Pig year of the fourth cycle of the Tibetan calendar (A.D. 1231), when the Yuan Emperor Xian Zong Monge Khan brought Tibet under the central government of our motherland. This period is called in the Tibetan annals "the Great Division of Tufan." The state of anarchy lasted altogether 393 years.

In the ninth year of the revolt of slaves and commoners, the Fire Cock year 1,421 years after the *parinirvana* of Sakyamuni (A.D. 877), Blon-po-shud-pu stag-rtse-gnyags and others decided to divide the tombs of all the btsan-pos among the six families of Gnyags, Zhur-bu, Khu, Snyi-ba, 'Bro, and Cog-ro. The result was that almost all the tombs were excavated, except that of Srong-btsan Sgam-po at 'Phyongs-rgyas and that of Mang-srong mang-btsan at Don-mkhar-mda (in modern 'Phyongs-rgyas County).

Mnga'-dbag-dpal-'khor-btsan, 'Od-srung's son, ruled over the Lho-kha region for eleven years and was killed in the Wood Hare year (A.D. 895), when he was thirty-one years old, by Blon-po-shud-pu stagrtse-gnyags, the chief of the slave uprising, in the fort of Myang-ro-sham-po.* His eldest son, Skyid-bde-nyi-ma-mgon, and second son, Khri-bkra-shis-brtsegs-pa-dpal, fled, the former to the Mnga'-ris region, and the latter to La-stod. Skyid-bde-nyi-ma-mgon in Mnga-ris had three sons. The eldest son, Dpal-sde-rig-pa-mgon, occupied Mon-yul and founded the

---

*According to the *Religious History of Myang*, it was the fort in the former Rgyal-rtse rdzong.

royal family of Ladakh;* the third son, Lde-gtsug-mgon, occupied Zhang-Zhung and founded the royal family of Gu-ge. Khri-bkra-shia-brtsegs-pa-dpal had three sons (Dpal-lde, 'Od-lde, and Skid'-lde), of whom the second son, 'Od-lde, had four sons (Pha-ba-de-se, Khri-lde, Kri-chung, and Nyag-pa). The descendants of Pha-ba-de-se and those of Nyag-pa became the lords at Rong myang-stod and Gyas-ru-byang in the Gtsang region. The second son, Khri-lde, fled to Mdo-smad (Chab-mdo, Khams) and finally settled down in Qinghai; and his descendants became leaders or members of the Rgyal-sras tribe. The third son, Kri-chung, remained at Yar-lung and founded the family of Yar-lung-jo-bo.

All the separatist aristocratic forces mentioned above engaged in long wars, which caused severe damage to agriculture and animal husbandry in Tibet. At the same time, natural disasters and famines hit Tibet one after another. So the masses of inhabitants in the Dbus and Gtsang regions had to emigrate to Mdo-Smad and other places where the economy was in better condition. During this period of anarchy, the people of Tufan suffered much from endless wars and natural disasters.

During the later period of the Tufan anarchy, in the Fire Rat year before the initiation of the Tibetan way of numbering years, 1,460 years after the *parinirvana* of Sakyamuni (A.D. 916), in the northeastern part of our country, Yelü Apochi, a leader of the Qidan (Khitan) nationality, unified all the Qidan groups and established a Qidan feudal regime called "Liao." His capital was near Balin Left Banner in the modern Liaoning Province. Liao had fourteen reigns.

The reign of the third and last emperor Gong Di of the Later Zhou of the Five Dynasties lasted for only three months. In the Earth Sheep year before the initiation of the Tibetan way of numbering years, 1,504 years after the *parinirvana* of Sakya-

---

*The second son, Bkra-shis-lde-mgon, occupied Pu-hrang, but his family lineage was not recorded in annals.

muni (A.D. 960), Zhao Kuangyin, a general of the Later Zhou, staged a coup d'état, overthrew the government, and established the Northern Song Dynasty, the capital of which was located at Kaifeng in Henan Province. He unified most of China with the exception of Liao and Western Xia to the north of the Yellow River. In the fifth year of the reign of the fourth emperor Ren Zong of the Northern Song, i.e., the Earth Tiger year of the Tibetan calendar (A.D. 1038), a minister named Li Yuanhao precipitated a rebellion and founded the Western Xia regime with its capital established at modern Yinchuan of Ningxia. Western Xia had ten reigns.

In the Wood Sheep year of the second cycle of the Tibetan calendar, 1,659 years after the *parinirvana* of Sakyamuni (A.D. 1115), Wanyan Aktta, a tribal chief of the Nüchen nationality, unified all tribes of Nüchen along the Songhua River and in the middle and lower reaches of the Heilong River. He founded the Kin Dynasty, located his capital city at Acheng in Heilongjiang Province, and later moved it to Kaifeng in Henan. The Kin Dynasty had nine reigns. In the Wood Snake year of the second cycle of the Tibetan calendar (A.D. 1125), the Song and Kin dynasties joined forces and wiped out Liao. The next year, Kin, taking advantage of Song's relaxing vigilance, wiped out the Song Dynasty in a sudden and violent attack. The Song Emperor Gao Zong fled to Zhejiang Province and founded the Southern Song Dynasty with Lin'an (modern Hangzhou) as its capital city. The Southern Song Dynasty had nine reigns and was finally wiped out by the Yuan Emperor Kublai Khan. Thus, China was reunified by the Yuan Dynasty.

8. The Revival of Buddhism in Tibet

In the Earth Tiger year prior to the initiation of the Tibetan way of numbering years, 1,522 years after the *parinirvana* of

Sakyamuni (A.D. 978), the "ten scholars of Dbus and Gtsang" arrived at Mdo-smad and were given full monastic ordination under the guidance of Grung Ye-shes-rgyal-mtshan, the disciple of Spa-gong Ye-shes-gyung-grung, who was the close disciple of the Great Master Dgongs-pa-rab-gsal. Later, they returned to the Dbus-gtsang region one after another. They dared not stay at Lhasa, and thus went to Bsam-yas. Among the Buddhist scholars of Dbus, Klu-mes Tshul-khrims-shes-rab became the abbot of the Ka-byung Temple; the two Rag-shi brothers became the abbots of the Dge-rgyas-bye-ma-gling Temple; 'Bring Ye-shes-yon-tan became the abbot of the Khams-gsum-zangs-khang-gling Temple, and Rba-Tshul-khrims-blo-gros and his brother became the abbots of the Bsam-yas Monastery. Later, they returned to the Lhasa region one after another. Since then, Klu-mes in the upper Dbus built the Chag-de'u Temple as his base. He had four favourite disciples, called the "Four Pillars." Among them, Zhang-sna-snang rdo-rje-dbang-phyugs founded the Rgyal-lug-glas Temple at 'Phan-po as his base, and developed the "group of Zhang"; Rngog Byang-chub-'byung-gnas founded the Yer-pa Temple at Yer-pa as his base and developed the "group of Rngog"; Glan Ye-shes-shes-rab founded the Rgya-gsar-sgang Temple as his base and developed the "group of Glan"; and Gru-mer Tshul-khrims-'byung-gnas founded the Thang-po-che Temple as his base and developed the "group of Thang." The four groups considered as a whole were called the "Klu-mes Group."

Rba Tshul-khrims-blo-gros, one of the five scholars of Dbus, founded the Lan-pa-spyil-bu Temple at Phan-po as his base and developed the "group of Rba." Rag-shi Tshul-khrims-dbang-phyugs of the five scholars of Dbus built the 'Phreng-'og-lha-khang Temple at Mal-gro as his base and developed the "group of Rag." 'Bring Ye-shes-yon-tan of the five scholars of Dbus built the Ngan-lam-rgyal-mo Temple as his base and developed the "group of 'Bring."

These four groups—Klu-mes, Rba, Rag, and 'Bring—gradually became stronger in Lhasa. Through the 11th century to the early 12th century, they clashed in a series of wars among themselves. In the Fire Dog year of the second cycle of the Tibetan calendar (A.D. 1106), the Klu-mes group fought with the Rba and Rag groups. As a result, a great part of the walls and chapels around the main hall of the Bsam-yas Monastery were destroyed. Later, Rdo-rje-grags, a sutra translator of the Rag group, had the monastery reconstructed in a period of two years by five hundred workers with a great amount of timber from 'Ol-kha; the expenditure on the reconstruction was equivalent to more than 100,000 *khal* of crops. All this was recorded in detail in the *Biography of Rdo-rje-grags, the Sutra Translator of the Rag Group* written by Rwa-chos-rab, the disciple of that translator.

In the Iron Dragon year of the third cycle of the Tibetan calendar (A.D. 1160), the four groups in Lhasa, Yar-lung and Phan-po engaged in a long period of wars with each other which caused serious damage to the Jokhang Temple, the Ramoche Temple, and the Khra-'brug Temple. Dwags-sgom Tshul-khrims-snying-po, the disciple of Dwags-po-lha-rje, mediated among the four groups. He had the Jokhang and the Ramoche temples in Lhasa repaired and then entrusted them to the custody of Gung-thang-lha-ma-zhang*, a personage influential in economic and military affairs of Lhasa. A description of this incident was given in the last part of the *ja* volume and the first part of the *na* volume of *The Religious History of Lho-brag* (Lho-brag-chos-byung), in the *zha* volume of *Blue Annals*, and in *The Religious History of Lho-rong* (Lho-rong-chos-byung).

The four newly developed groups mentioned above were not different in religious doctrines. They fought with one another only to obtain more economic benefits and property.

---

*The founder of the Tshal-pa Bka'-brgyud sect.

Their wars not only resulted in severe damage to agricultural and pastoral production and in great loss of lives and property of the people, but also caused much destruction of the Jokhang Temple, the Ramoche Temple, the Khra-'brug Temple, and the Bsam-yas Monastery, which had been constructed by the ancient Tibetan people in their wisdom and with their superb skills and techniques. It was obviously the fact that the monks could not get rid of their parasitic way of life that led them to fight with each other for economic benefits.

Thirty years after the formation of these four groups, in the Iron Dragon year of the first cycle of the Tibetan calendar (A.D. 1040), Lha-bla-ma Byang-chub-'od of Gu-ge in the Mnga'-ris region invited Atisha from India to Tibet. Atisha spent seventeen years preaching Buddhism in Mnga'-ris, Lhasa, Snye-thang, Brag-yel-pa, 'Phan-po, and other Tibetan areas. Three years after his death, in the Fire Cock year of the first cycle of the Tibetan calendar (A.D. 1057), his disciple 'Brom-ston-pa rgyal-bai-byung-gnas built the Rva-sgreng Monastery and became its abbot. Thus the Bka'-gdams sect was founded. The donors for the building of the monastery were Yon-bdag sha-kamgon and 'Zhang-'phrang kha-ber-chung.

Sixteen years later, in the Water Ox year of the first cycle of the Tibetan calendar (A.D. 1073), 'Khon dkon-chog rgyal-po built Sa-skya Monastery and became its abbot. Thus the Sa-skya sect was founded.

Forty-eight years later, in the Iron Ox year of the second cycle of the Tibetan calendar (A.D. 1121), Mkhas-grub-khyung-po-rnal-'byor built the Zhang-zhung Temple as his base. And thus the Shangs-pa Bka'-brgyud sect was founded.

In the same year, Dwags-po-lha-rje, the disciple of Mi-la-ras-pa, built the Dwags-lha-sgam-po Temple as his base. And thus was founded the Dwags-po Bka'-brgyud sect.

Thirty-seven years later, in the Earth Tiger year of the third cycle of the Tibetan calendar (A.D. 1158), Phag-mo-gru-pa rdo-rje-rgyal-po, a disciple of Dwags-po-lha-rje, built Phag-mo-gru Monastery as his base. And thus was founded the Phag-gru Bka'-brgyud sect.

Two years later, in the Iron Dragon year of the third cycle of the Tibetan calendar (A.D. 1160), 'Bab-ram-pa dar-ma-dbang-phyug, a disciple of Phag-mo-gru-pa, built the 'Bab-ram-ri-bo-che Temple in the Nagchu region as his base. And thus was founded the 'Bab-ram Bka-brgyud sect.

Seven years later, in the Fire Pig year of the third cycle of the Tibetan calendar (A.D. 1167), Smar-ba shes-rab-ye-shes, a disciple of Phag-mo-gru-pa, built the Zhod-dyon Temple in the central part of the Khams region as his base. And thus was founded the Smar-pa Bak'-brgyud sect.

Four years later, in the Iron Hare year of the third cycle of the Tibetan calendar (A.D. 1171), Sangs-rgyas-yel-pa ye-shes-brtsegs, a disciple of Phag-mo-gru-pa, built the Yel-phug Monastery in the Khams region and became its abbot. And thus was founded the Yel-phug Bka'-brgyud sect.

In the same year, Rgal-tsha-rin-chen-mgon, a disciple of Phag-mo-gru-pa, built the Khro-phug Monastery in the Gtsang region as his base. And thus was founded the Khro-phug Bka'-brgyud sect.

Four years later, in the Wood Sheep year of the third cycle of the Tibetan calendar (A.D. 1175), Gung-thang-lha-ma Zhang-brtson-grags-pa, a disciple of Dvags-sgom tshul-khrims snying-po (a disciple of Dwags-po-lha-rje) built the Tshal-pa Monastery as his base. And thus was founded the Tshal-pa Bka'-brgyud sect.

Four years later, in the Earth Pig year of the third cycle of the Tibetan calendar (A.D. 1179), Skyob-pa 'jig-rten-mgon-po, a disciple of Phag-mo-gru-pa, built the 'Bri-gung-mthil Monastery as his base. And thus was founded the Bri-gung Bka'-brgyud sect.

The next year, Stag-lung-thang-pa bkra-shis-dpal, a disciple of Phag-mo-gru-pa, built Stag-lung Monastery as his settlement. And thus was founded the Stag-lung Bka'brgyud sect.

A year later, in the Iron Ox year of the third cycle of the Tibetan calendar (A.D. 1181), Gyer-sgom-pa tshul-khrims-seng-ge, a disciple of Phag-mo-gru-pa, built the Gseb-phu-shug-gseb Monastery as his base. And thus was founded the Shug-gseb Bka'-brgyud sect.

Eight years later, in the Earth Cock year of the third cycle of the Tibetan calendar (A.D. 1189), Karma-pa dus-sum-mkhyen-pa, a disciple of Dwags-po-lha-rje, built Mtshur-phur Monastery and became its abbot. And thus was founded the Karma Bka'-brgyud sect.

Four years later, in the Water Ox year of the third cycle of the Tibetan calendar (A.D. 1193), 'Gro-mgon-gtsang-pa-rgya-ras, a disciple of Gling-ras-pa padma-rdo-rje (a disciple of Phag-mo-gru-po), built the 'Brug-ra-lung Monastery as his base. And thus was founded the 'Brug-pa Bka-brgyud sect.

Thirteen years later, in the Fire Tiger year of the third cycle of the Tibetan calendar (A.D. 1206), Gya'-bzang-ba-chos-smon-lam, a disciple of Za-ra-ba skal-ldan-ye-shis-seng-ge (a disciple of Phag-mo-gru-pa), built the Gya'-bzang Monastery as his base. And thus was founded the Gya'-bzang Bka'-brgyud sect.

Excepting the Bka'-gdams, Sa-skya, and Shang-pa-bka'-rgyud sects, the sects mentioned above were called Bka'-brgyud-pa as a whole. Bka'-brgyud-pa consisted of four main groups and eight subgroups. The main groups were (1) Tshal-pa Bka'-brgyud sect, (2) Phag-gru Bka'-brgyud sect, (3) 'Bab-ram Bka'-brgyud sect, and (4) Karma Bka'-brgyud sect. They upheld directly the tradition of Dwags-po-lha-rje and were therefore called "main groups." The subgroups were (1) Bri-gung Bka'-brgyud sect, (2) Stag-lung Bka'-brgyud sect, (3) Khro-phug Bka'-brgyud sect, (4) 'Brug-pa Bka'-brgyud sect, (5) Smar-ba Bka'-brgyud sect, (6) Yel-pa Bka'-brgyud sect, (7) Gya'-bzang Bka'-brgyud sect, and (8) Shug-gseb Bka'-brgyud sect. They upheld directly the tradition of Phag-mo-gru-pa, the disciple of Dwags-po-lha-rhe, and were therefore called "subgroups." The founders of these various religious sects occupied a place of their own, had a monastery built there as their base, and gradually expanded their sphere of influence. Thus each subgroup developed into a local religious force. The first monastery they built as their base was called the main monastery, and the monasteries built later were called "submonasteries."

During a period of 150 years, from the year of the Fire Cock of the first cycle of the Tibetan calendar (A.D. 1057) to the year of the Fire Tiger of the third cycle (A.D. 1206), various religious sects emerged one after another in Tibet as a result of both internal and external conditions.

Tibet's internal conditions. By the middle period of Tufan anarchy, the system of Tibetan feudal economy had already struck roots in the Tibetan society, agricultural and pastoral productivity grew rapidly, and handicraft and trade flourished. In Ding-ri and Gya'-lam of the western Mnga'-ris region, and Lha-rtse of the Gtsang region, marketplaces had already begun to appear. In Gu-ge of the western Mnga'-ris and Lo-rdeng in the northern Gtsang, gold mines had been opened up. In Lho-kha and Ngam-ring, the ceramic industry had begun to develop.

As recorded in some annals, at that time the price of a horse was 4 *khal* of grain. As for gold and silver, the system of weight measure and price ratio went as follows: the weight of a jequirity bean* was 1 *se-ba*, 8 *se-ba* was equal to 1 *qian*, and 8 *qian* was equal to 1 tael. One tael of gold was equal to 2 taels of silver, and 4 taels of gold (8 taels of Tibetan silver) was called an ingot of silver. Sixteen taels of gold was called an ingot of gold, equivalent to 2 ingots of silver. A big ingot of silver was equal to 50 taels of silver or 25 taels of gold. Weights were

---

*This bean is called *dmar-ru-mgo-nag* in Tibetan and is always used as weight.

measured by steelyards, which were made of wood.

For medicines and crops, the measurement of capacity was divided into six units. The smallest unit was *kham-tshig*, 6 *kham-tshig* were equal to 1 *star-phul*, 6 *star-phul* to 1 *bya-sgong*, 6 *bya-sgong* to 1 *mkharphul*, 6 *mkharphul* to 1 *shen*, 20 *shen* to 1 *khal*. The records of these weights and measures can be found in the medical books and the explanatory notes to the Buddhist commandments of that time. As compared with the measurement of crops and medicines by handfuls in the time of Srong-btsan Sgam-po, the system of measurement by this time had progressed greatly.

There were now six measure units for Tibetan medicines and yak butter. The smallest unit was 1 *se-ba* (the weight of 6 grains of barley), 20 *se-ba* were equal to 1 *qian*, 10 *qian* were equal to 1 tael (also called *spor*), 4 taels or 4 *spor* were equal to 1 *nya-ka*, 5 *nya-ka* to 1 *khyor*, 20 *khyor* to 1 *khal*. A detailed description of this system can be found in some books of Tibetan medicine of that time.

In the middle period of Tibetan anarchy 153 Buddhist translators went to India, three times as many as in the first diffusion of Buddhism.* In the closing years of the period of the great division, seventy-three panditas from India, Pakistan, Afghanistan, and Kashmir came to Tibet—three times as many as in the first diffusion of Buddhism.** The Tibetan translators who went to India, Nepal, or Kashmir generally spent at least seven years there, some even twenty years. They had to take with them enough gold to pay for one to three years' tuition and personal expenses. When they exhausted their money, they came back, tried to get more gold, and went abroad again. If the 153 translators who went abroad during the second diffusion of

---

*Fifty-one translators went to India to study in the period of the first diffusion of Buddhism.

**Twenty-two panditas came to Tibet from abroad in the period of the first diffusion of Buddhism.

Buddhism studied for an average of nine years, spending eighty taels of gold for each year's expenses, then totally they would have taken abroad 110,160 taels of gold.

Tibet's external conditions. In the Iron Dragon year of the first cycle of the Tibetan calendar (A.D. 1040), Atisha came to Tibet. Not long after that, Arabian troops from Stag-gzig (the name of Persia in Tibetan) occupied most of India, excepting the southern part. This put Islamism in a dominant position in central India, while the influential force of Buddhism began to decay. But in Burma, Kampuchea, Laos, and Thailand, Buddhism still enjoyed its authority.

More than 160 years later, in the Iron Cock year of the third cycle (A.D. 1201), the Arabian army occupied the whole of central, southern, and western India. Most of the Indian Buddhist scholars and monks escaped to Burma, Vietnam, Laos, Kampuchea, and Thailand, and a small group of them went through Assam and Nepal to Tibet. The famous scholar in Tibetan history Kha-che-pan-chen Sha-kya-shiri (Sa-skya-pan-chen's teacher) was one of them. He had been living in the northern border region of India, and in the Wood Rat year of the third cycle (A.D. 1204), on the invitation of Byams-pa-dpal (a Tibetan translator), he came to Tibet by way of Yadong. He lived in Tibet for ten years, preaching Buddhism enthusiastically. He began to write *Chronicles of Buddhism* in the third month of the Fire Hare year of the fourth cycle. The following year, he arrived in the Gtsang region and lived at the Myang-smad-can-gong Monastery. At that time, Sha-kya-pan-chen, at the age of twenty-seven, joined the *bhikchu* monkhood under the guidance of Kha-che-pan-chen and founded a new *bhikchu* precept tradition called the "Kha-che-pan-chen precept tradition." Hence there were now altogether four sets of precepts.*

While declining in India, Buddhism revived in Tibet. This

---

*They are called Bye-rdzing-pa, Chen-pa, Dge-'dun-sgang-pa, and Tshal-mig-pa.

period in Tibetan history is called "the diffusion of Buddhism from India to the north." Later, Buddhism had a further expansion through Gansu and Qinghai to Inner Mongolia and Kharkha (Outer Mongolia). In Tibetan annals, this is called "the diffusion of Buddhism from the northern land to the north." For a period of 392 years (A.D. 846-1238), from the time when Glang-dar-ma proscribed Buddhism through the Tufan anarchy to the unification of Tibet by Yuan Emperor Xian Zong, Monge Khan, both the local regime of Tibet and the central political power in the hinterland of our country were all split up. The various Buddhist sects that emerged and developed in Tibet were local religious groups backed by local political forces. They enhanced political chaos and were the basic reason why Tibet could not be unified for a very long time. Besides, as has been mentioned above, in the time of *btsan-po* Khri-srong-lde-btsan, monks owned slave households and received daily necessities from the *btsan-po*'s storehouse, but in the time of Khri-ral-pa-can, they were assigned farms, pastureland and livestock for their support. Here we see two quite different institutions. If the upper-ranking religious personages owned only slave households and got the means of subsistence from the royal storehouse but were not given any farms, pastureland, or livestock, then they were slave owners only and would not have become landlords. Had the monks not owned any farms, pastureland, and livestock, they would not have attempted to attain political power to protect their economic base and their ownership of productive means. Had the monks not had any desire for power, Tibet would not have developed a system of local regimes based on an amalgamation of temporal and spiritual government under which the Buddhist personages of upper strata held the power. Nevertheless, owing to extremely low productivity, the *btsan-po* could finance only a small number of monks. When the supply for the increased number of monks exceeded the financial capacity of the local government, it became a burden to the royal family, officials, and people. To solve this problem, the local government had no alternative but to relinguish responsibility for the monks' daily necessities and assign them farms, pastureland, and livestock for their maintenance. In this way, the monks' resources for living were ensured. The financial strength of the upper-ranking religious personages became stronger and stronger. Finally, some of them became powerful landlords owning a vast expanse of land, pastureland, and livestock. This was the class base for the formation of the Tibetan polity based on a merger of secular and clerical rule.

II. The Establishment of the Politico-Religious Institution and the Struggle for Political Power Among the Elites of Various Religious Sects

1. The Monopoly of the Sa-skya Sect of the Tibetan Local Political Power and the War Between the Sa-skya Sect and the Bri-goug Bka'-brgyud Sect

In the Earth Cock year of the third cycle of the Tibetan calendar (A.D. 1189), Genghis Khan, having unified all Mongolian tribes, began his expeditions to Central Asia, West Asia, and East Europe. After conquering the foreign enemies, he waged a war to unify China, putting a great part of the country under his domination except the territories of the Western Xia regime, the Southern Song Dynasty, and the Kin Dynasty. At that time, the various Tibetan religious sects and political groups had not yet achieved unification. Genghis Khan took the opportunity to send troops to the Dbus-Gtsang region in the Fire Tiger year of the third cycle of the Tibetan calendar (A.D. 1206). The chiefs in the Dbus, Gtsang, and Mnga'-ris regions dared not resist and promised to give allegiance to the Mongols. The lamas of the Sa-skya sect were the first to establish contact with the Mongols.* They took a great number of Buddha statues

---

*Sum-pa mkhan-po ye-shes dpal-'byor's *History of the Treasure Tree of Buddhism*, Pan-chen Bsod-nams Grags-pa's *New Red Annals* (also called *A Divine Key to the Royal Lineage*), and many other Tibetan annals say that when Genghis Khan dispatched troops into Tibet, Sde-sri jo-dga', Tshal-pa kun-dga' rdo-rje, and many others gave their allegiance to the Mongols, and that the Mongols established contact with the Sa-skya hierarch Kun-dga' snying-po. Such a statement is wrong.

and sutras from the Dbus-Gtsang region to Mongol areas, and this was the beginning of the introduction of Buddhism into Mongolia. Genghis Khan conquered the Western Xia regime in the Fire Pig year of the fourth cycle of the Tibetan calendar (A.D. 1227). After he had a talk on Buddhism with Dung-khur-ba Dbang-phyug-bkra-shis, the spiritual teacher of the king of the Western Xia and a Tibetan lama of the Tshal-pa Bka'-brgyud sect, he decreed in the *Edict on According Courteous Reception to the Monks* that the Tibetan monks be exempted from taxes and military service, and he bestowed many privileges on them.

But at that time, different religious groups had their own spheres of influence. Although they owned vast expanses of land and pastureland, and had livestock, slave and subjects, the political powers they relied on were different. The only way in which a religious faction could consolidate and expand its power and influence was to seek the patronage of a very strong political, economic, and military power. So in the Earth Pig year of the fourth cycle of the Tibetan calendar (A.D. 1239), all sects, including the Sa-skya sect, Phag-mo-gru-pa sect, Bri-gung sect, Tshal-pa sect, stag-lung sect, and G.ya'-bzang sect, sent their representatives to the Mongol areas. The Sa-skya sect gave its allegiance to Ogadai Khan. Both the Phag-mo-gru sect and the G.ya'-bzang sect gave their allegiance to Prince Hulagu. The Bri-gung sect and the Gtsang-gur-mo sect gave allegiance to Prince Kublai, while the Stag-lung sect gave allegiance to Prince Arikboga. The khan and the princes gave the sects land and subjects, the areas of land and numbers of subjects being similar to those they had had before. There were 2,438 households on the land Hulagu bestowed on the Phag-mo-gru-pa sect, 2,630 households on the land Monge Khan bestowed on the Bri-gung sect, 3,700 households on the land Kublai Khan bestowed on the Tshal-pa sect, 3,000 households on the land prince Hulagu bestowed on the G.ya-bzang sect, and 500 households on the land Arikboga bestowed on the Stag-lung sect. The land prince Go-dan bestowed on the Sa-skya sect included seven *wan-hu* (meaning "ten thousand households")—La-stod-lho, La-stod-byang, Gur-mo, Chu-mig, Shangs, Zha-lu, and Yar-'brog—the households on which amounted to 10,885.

In the following year, the Iron Rat year of the fourth cycle of the Tibetan calendar (A.D. 1240), Prince Go-dan sent an expeditionary force under General Dor-rta-nag-po's command to Tibetan areas. In the Wood Dragon year of the fourth cycle of the Tibetan calendar (A.D. 1244), Prince Go-dan of the Yuan Dynasty invited Sa-skya Pandita to the hinterland.

In the Water Rat year of the fourth cycle of the Tibetan calendar (A.D. 1252), Monge Khan ascended the throne. In the following year, the Water Ox year (A.D. 1253), he sent troops to Tibet and merged it into China's territory. In the Wood Hare year of the fourth cycle of the Tibetan calendar (A.D. 1255), Kublai invited Karma Pakshi Chos-kyi bla-ma, leader and second Living Buddha of the Karma Bka'-brgyud sect, to the hinterland. Hence the Karma Bka'-brgyud sect established contacts with the Yuan court.

In the Iron Monkey year of the fourth cycle of the Tibetan calendar (A.D. 1260), Kublai ascended the throne. He invited 'Phags-pa to the hinterland for the second time. The first time 'Phags-pa had gone to the hinterland was in 1244, when he accompanied his uncle Sa-skya Pandita to Liangzhou. Kublai treated Karma pakshi and 'Phags-pa as his spiritual instructors. In the Wood Ox year of the fourth cycle (A.D. 1265), 'Phags-pa was asked to hold a Tantric *Murddhabhichikta* (meaning "washing the top of the head") ceremony for Kublai Khan. For this Kublai Khan bestowed on 'Phags-pa thirteen *wan-hu*. Later on, the emperor of the Yuan Dynasty in the year of the Earth Dragon of the fifth cycle (A.D. 1268) dispatched two imperial envoys, A-kon and Mi-gling, to Tibet to take a census of the population for the first time. In the Fire Pig year twenty years later (A.D. 1287) the emperor of the Yuan Dynasty dispatched imperial envoy Do-su-a-nu-gan to Tibet to take a second census of the population together with *Dpon-chen* Gzhun-nu-dbang-phyug. According to *Sa-skya gdung-rabs* (Sa-skya's Lineal Description), the Yuan court stipulated that a family with a man and a wife, two children, two servants, a horse, a mule, a goat, a sheep, an ox, a *pien niu* (offspring of a bull and a female yak), a house with six stanchions, and a piece of arable land on which 12 *khal* of seeds could be sown constituted a *dud-chung*. Twenty five *dud-chung* constituted a *dud-chen*, two *dud-chen* constituted one *rta-mgo*, two *rta-mgo* constituted one *bai-hu* (100 households), ten *bai-hu* constituted one *qian-hu* (1,000 households), ten *qian-hu* constituted one *wan-hu*. According to this stipulation, thirteen *wan-hu* should have had 130,000 households with a population of 780,000 and 130,000 head of each kind of domestic animal. But at that time Tibet was sparsely populated. The actual number of households in each *wan-hu* was as follows:

(1) La-stod-lho *wan-hu*, 2,250 households

(2) La-stod-byang *wan-hu*, 2,250 households

(3) Chu-mig *wan-hu*, 3,003 households

(4) Gur-mo *wan-hu*, 750 households

(5) Zha-lu *wan-hu*, 3,892 households

(6) Shangs *wan-hu*, 1,400 households

(7) Rgya-ma *wan-hu*, 5,950 households

(8) Phag-gru *wan-hu*, 2,438 households

(9) Bri-gung *wan-hu*, 3,630 households

(10) Tshal-pa *wan-hu*, 3,700 households

(11) Bya-yul *wan-hu*, 5,950 households

(12) Yar-'brog *wan-hu*, 750 households

(13) G.ya-bzang *wan-hu*, 3,000 households

Tshal-pa Kun-dga' rdo-rje, the author of the *Red Annals*, was born in the Earth Cock year of the fifth cycle of the Tibetan calendar (A.D. 1309) and died in the Water Serpent year of the sixth cycle (A.D. 1353). He allied himself with Bri-gung-pa to attack Ta-si-thu byang-chub rgyal-mtshan, but he lost the battle and surrendered all his power to Ta-si-thu. Ta-si-thu gave a detailed account of this incident in his own book *A Collection of Deceased Kings' Teachings*, and Tshal-pa Kun-dga' rdo-rje also talked about this incident in his *Red Annals*. Genghis Khan was born in the Water Horse year of the third cycle of the Tibetan calendar (A.D. 1162) and died in the Fire Pig year of the fourth cycle (A.D. 1227). Tshal-pa Kun-dga' rdo-rje was not contemporary with Genghis Khan.

It was in the Fire Tiger year of the third cycle (A.D. 1206), that Genghis Khan dispatched troops into Tibet. By that time Sa-skya Dpon-chen Kun-dga' snying-po had already been dead for forty-eight years, and Sa-skya Dpon-chen Bsod-nams-rtse-mo for twenty-five years. Rje-btsun Grags-pa rgyal-mtshan at the time was sixty years old. So, it is obvious that the Sa-skya hierarch with whom Genghis Khan established contact was not Sa-skya Dpon-chen Kun-dga' snying-po, but Rje-btsun Grags-pa rgyal-mtshan.

The total number of households was therefore 38,963. If there were six people in a household, there would have been altogether 233,778 people. *Sa-skya's Lineal Description* also states that, as the donation offered for his second Tantric *Murddhabhichikta* ritual, Kublai bestowed on 'Phags-pa three Tibetan regions, the population and area of which were less than those of a province. *The Analects on the Historical Relations Between the Hans and Tibetans* says that when Kublai asked 'Phags-pa to hold the third Tantric *Murddhabhichikta* ritual for him, 'Phags-pa requested that he abolish the practice of drowning the Hans. According to *The Biography of 'Phags-pa* after Genghis Khan conquered the Han areas, the Han people often rose in revolt. So troops were sent every year to capture the Hans by the thousands and drown them in the Yellow River. At that time the Yellow River was full of corpses and blood and the sky was said to have become red from its reflection. But after 'Phags-pa presided over the *Murddhabhichikta* ritual for Kublai, the practice of drowning the Hans stopped.

In the Water Monkey year of the fifth cycle of the Tibetan calendar (A.D. 1272), the Yuan court set up in Tibet an administrative organization called the Tufan Pacification Commissioner's Office, established post stations and military stations and began to levy a certain amount of taxes on Tibetans.

During the ninety-one years from the Wood Ox year of the fourth cycle of the Tibetan calendar (A.D. 1264) to the Wood Horse year of the sixth cycle (A.D. 1354), there were altogether nine Sa-skya hierarchs (from 'Phags-pa down to Ta-dben Blo-gros-rgyal-mtshan) and twenty *dpon-chen* (from *dpon-chen* Shak-ya Bzang-po down to *dpon-chen* Dbang-brtson). Under the direct jurisdiction of the Yuan Dynasty central government, they ruled over the whole of Tibet and became the leaders in charge of Tibetan secular as well as religious affairs. This shows that high-ranking Buddhist monks occupied a dominant position not only in economic affairs but also in political affairs, and that they had risen from landlord class to a ruling class in political affairs. Furthermore, this shows that Buddhism could not break away from politics and act independently.

'Phags-pa was the supreme leader of the three kinds of feudal lords of Tibet at that time. Under him an administrative apparatus of various levels was established. It included the high official *dpon-chen*, who was in charge of all administrative affairs; the chiefs of *wan-hu*; the chiefs of *qian-hu;* the *rdzong-dpon*, an official in charge of a fort or district; and the stewards of manorial estates. In addition to this, thirteen kinds of new official posts whose aim was to serve high-ranking monks personally were set up for the first time. They were:

Gsol-dpon, attendants in charge of high-ranking monks' daily life, clothes, etc.

Gzim-dpon, officials in charge of high-ranking monks' food

Mchod-dpon, officials in charge of high-ranking monks' sutras and sacrificial offerings

Mgron-gnyer, officials in charge of receiving guests and transmitting orders;

Drung-yig, officials in charge of writing out and copying letters and preserving documents and files

Phyyag-mdzod, officials in charge of financial affairs

Ma-chen, attendants in charge of serving tea

Sger-dpon, heads of a village or leaders of a caravan

Gdan-gnyer, officials in charge of serving seats and cushions

Khang-gnyer, officials in charge of house management

Chibs-dpon, officials in charge of horses or mules

Sgar-pa, guards at the entrance

A-drung, messengers

Thus a whole set of religious and political administrative systems of the ruling class was established. General local administrative affairs were conducted by the Sa-skya hierarch and *dpon-chen*, but the conduct of more important affairs and the appointment and removal of a *dpon-chen* had to be reported to the Yuan central government and could not be carried out until it had been approved by the central government. Most *dpon-chen*s were directly appointed by the Yuan central government. From the foregoing, the following four conclusions can be drawn:

(1) The Tibetan polity, which was based on the merging of religious and secular rule and in which high-ranking Buddhist monks acted as religious and political leaders, began to emerge at the time when 'Phags-pa took control of the Tibetan local regime.

(2) The rise of high-ranking monks from the economic landlord class to the political ruling class also began during this period.

(3) The Sa-skya sect did not control the Tibetan local regime independently or have the initiative in its own hands, but

was under the direct jurisdiction of the Yuan central government.

(4) The monks in the upper strata of the Sa-skya sect, in order to consolidate and develop their own influence, needed the Yuan court to patronize them politically; on the other hand, the Yuan court needed the monks in the upper strata of the Sa-skya sect to strengthen its political power and to consolidate its supremacy over Tibet. Only owing to these two factors did the Sa-skya sect become the leader of both political and religious circles.

From the Wood Ox year of the fourth cycle of the Tibetan calendar (A.D. 1264) 'Phags-pa assumed the reins of government for three years. Then he appointed Shakya Bzang-po as *dpon-chen* and appointed his own stepbrother Rin-chen-rgyal-mtshan as acting Sa-skya hierarch before he himself went to the hinterland for the second time. In the Iron Horse year of the fifth cycle of the Tibetan calendar (A.D. 1270), 'Phags-pa elaborated a new Mongolian script based on Tibetan writing. It was later called the "'Phags-pa script." In recognition of his service, Emperor Kublai conferred on him the title of "The Only One in the World, Incarnate Buddha, Protector of the State's Polity, Composer of Writings, Origin of Learning, the Holy State Tutor," together with a jade seal symbolic of authority. At that time Kublai had thought of abolishing all the other sects in Tibet except the Sa-skya sect, but 'Phags-pa said to the emperor: "Except the Bon religion, all the Buddhist sects are of Buddhism, although their teaching systems are not the same. If other sects are not permitted to follow their own teaching system, it would not only reflect on Your Majesty's policy and prestige, but also do harm to the Sa-skya sect, so it is desirable to let all sects follow their own teaching systems." Kublai found 'Phags-pa's proposal fair and reasonable, so he decreed that all Biddhist sects of Tibet could freely develop their teaching systems and pray for the emperor's longevity. The freedom of religious belief of different sects is not only the basis of the unity of various sects, but also the basis of the internal and external unity of various nationalities. This farsighted proposal of 'Phags-pa did much good for the consolidation of the ruling power and prestige of the Yuan court, for the unity between the Tibetans and Mongols, for the internal unity of the Tibetan people, and for the maintenance of peace and stability in Tibet. This is why so many Tibetan historians have chanted the praises of 'Phags-pa. After 'Phags-pa left for the hinterland, his step-brother Rin-chen-rgyal-mtshan acted for the Sa-skya hierarch for thirteen years beginning in the Fire Hare year of the fifth cycle of the Tibetan calendar (A.D. 1267), and then was invited to the hinterland as successor to 'Phags-pa.

Later, Dharma-pa-la rakshi-ta, 'Phags-pa's brother Phyag-na rdo-rje's son, assumed the post of Sa-skya hierarch for eight years beginning in the year of the Iron Dragon of the fifth cycle (A.D. 1280). In the second year of his reign, the 12th *spyam-snga* (district governor) of the Bri-gung sect Rin-chen rdo-rje died at Bri-gung and Rim-po-che Grags-pa-ye-shes succeeded to his post. Grags-pa-ye-shes sent his own nephew Snag-tsha-grags-she-pa to visit Ye-shes-rim-chen, a lama of the Sa-skya sect. The Sa-skya sect was going to appoint Snag-tsha-grags-she-pa as abbot of the Bri-gung Monastery, but he was assassinated by Rgya-bo grags-pa-rin-chen, the brother of the 12th *spyan-snga* of the Bri-gung sect Rin-chen rdo-rje. When the Sa-skya sect denounced Rgya-bo grags-pa-rin-chen for his crime, all the monks of the Bri-gung sect stood up to support him. Hence the disputes and warfare between the Sa-skya sect and the Bri-gung sect began. In the fifth year of the reign of Dharma-pa-la rakshi-ta, the Wood Cock year of the fifth cycle (A.D. 1285), Kun-rdo-rin-chen of the Bri-gung sect invited Hulagu's 90,000 soldiers from western Mongolia into Tibet to attack the Sa-skya sect.*

Later, from the Fire Pig year of the fifth cycle (A.D. 1287), 'Jam-dbyangs-rin-chen-rgyal-mtshan, who was not of the Sa-skya family, became the ruler of Tibet for eight years. In the fourth year of his reign, Dbang-len, the *dpon-chen* of Sa-skya, invited the troops of Kublai's son Timur back into Tibet. Together with the Gtsang troops they attacked the Bri-gung sect, burnt down the main hall in the Bri-gung-mthil Monastery, and killed more than ten thousand monks and lay people. Territories which belonged to the Bri-gung sect, such as Byar, Dwags-po, Kong-po, E, Snye, Lho-ro Lho-kha, Brag-dkar, Ya-rgyab, and Mon, were captured by the Sa-skya sect. This incident is called Bri-gung-gling-log (the turmoil of the Bri-gung monasteries) in Tibetan historical records. Thus the Dbus and Gtsang regions began diametrically to oppose each other. The main reasons for their discord were as follows: (1) the doctrines and the teaching systems of the Sa-skya and Bri-gung sects were different; (2) the Gtsang and Stod regions were Sa-skya territory, while Dbus, Dwags-po, Kong-po, and other places mentioned above were Bri-gung territory; (3) the Sa-skya's patron was Kublai, while the Bri-gung sect's patron was Hulagu.

While the Sa-skya and the Bri-gung sects were fighting for manorial estates and slaves, they both flaunted the banner of religion and nationality and instigated their own patrons to dispatch Mongol troops into Tibet. The war between the Dbus and Gtsang regions not only created internal discord and contradictions among the Tibetan people in these two regions, but also created discord among the Mongol people and between the Tibetan and Mongol peoples. Many Tibetan historical records say that after the war between the Sa-skya sect and the Bri-gung sect broke out, relations between the Dbus and the Gtsang were

---

*Some people say the Mongolian troops which helped the Bri-gung sect to attack the Sa-skya sect could not have been Hulagu's soldiers. This remains to be verified.

like those "between a crow and an owl"—that is, they were bitter enemies. This is a simplified explanation of the contradictions between the Dbus and Gtsang people caused by the ruling circles of the Sa-skya and the Bri-gung sects. The religious personages in the upper strata, in order to expand their economic and political sphere of influence, would flaunt the banner of religion and nationality and, relying on their religious power, try to create discord and contradictions and thus instigate wars among the Tibetan people. In the ensuing sections we shall continue to discuss wars between different religious sects during various periods. Except for differences in the forms of struggle, the characters of the wars were the same as that described above, i.e., the combatants posed as spokesmen for their religion and nationality in order to seize economic benefits and political power. Therefore, we shall describe the wars between Buddhist sects in terms of the focal point of the contradictions of the various periods.

Bdag-chen bzang-po-dpal became the ruler of Tibet for nineteen years beginning in the Fire Horse year of the fifth cycle (A.D. 1306). He married Mon-ta-kham, the sister of Yuan Emperor Cheng Zong Timur; she bore him a son named Bsod-nams-bzang-po, who was later granted the title *Bailan king*. Bdag-chen bzang-po-dpal had seven wives and many sons. After he died, the Imperial Tutor Kun-dga' blo-gros (son of his second wife Ma-gcig-ngang-mo), assigned his brothers into four *bla brang**: (1) his brother Mkhas-brtsun nam-mkha' legs-pa was Bzhi-thog *bla brang* with a jade seal; (2) his brother the Imperial Tutor Kun-dga' legs-pa' byung-gnas was Lha-khang *bla brang* with a gold seal; (3) his brother 'Jam-dbyang don-yod rgyal-mtshan was Rin-chen *bla-brang* with a jade seal; (4) his brother Dbang kun-dga' legs-pa was Dud-mchod *bla-brang* with a gold seal. Not long after this, all the *bla-brangs* were in discord

---

* *Bla-brang*: Living Buddha's residential quarter.

with each other.

Mkhas-brtsun nam-mkha' legs-pa came into power for eighteen years beginning in the Wood Ox year of the fifth cycle (A.D. 1243). The Yuan Emperor Tai Ding Ye-sun-thi-mur conferred on him the honorific title "State Tutor of *Murddhabhi-chikta*" together with a jade seal symbolic of authority.

Later, 'Jam-dbyang don-yod rgyal-mtshan came into power for three years beginning in the Water Sheep year of the sixth cycle (A.D. 1343). The Yuan Emperor Shun Di Thu-hun-thi-mur conferred on him the honorific title "Great Yuan State Tutor" together with a jade seal symbolic of authority.

Later, Dam-pa bsod-nams rgyal-mtshan came into power for three years beginning in the Wood Cock year of the sixth cycle (A.D. 1345). The Yuan Dynasty Emperor Shun Di Thu-hun-thi-mur invited him four times to the capital city of Dadu (modern Beijing), but he declined.

Later, Ta-dben blo-gros rgyal-mtshan came into power for three years beginning in the Fire Pig year of the sixth cycle (A.D. 1347). In the first year of his reign, the Yuan Dynasty Emperor Shun Di Thu-hun-thi-mur conferred on him the honorific title of "Tuolin Minister, the Great Yuan State Tutor" together with a jade seal.

2. The Phag-gru Sect's Control of the Tibetan Local Regime and the Rise of the Dge-lugs Sect

In the Earth Ox year of the sixth cycle (A.D. 1349), the inner struggle between the four *bla-grang* became more severe and the Sa-skya sect divided into two groups: one was the Lha-khang *bla-grang* with *dpon-chen* Dbang-phyug-brtson-'grus as its head, and the other group was formed by the other three *bla-grang* with *dpon-chen* Rgyal-ba-bzang-po as its head. The latter was defeated in the struggle, and the brothers of the

Sa-skya family persecuted and killed each other. By that time, Byang-chub rgyal-mtshan, the head of the Phag-gru *wan-hu*, had defeated and eliminated the Bri-gung sect. Now he went over to *dpon-chen* Rgyal-ba-bzang-po's side and launched an attack on *dpon-chen* Dbang-phyug-brtson-'grus's group, the stronger section of the Sa-skya sect. The result was that the Sa-skya regime fell into the hands of the Phag-gru sect.

From the Earth Ox year of the sixth cycle (A.D. 1349) Byang-chub rgyal-mtshan was at the helm of the regime for sixteen years. In the fifth year of his reign, the Wood Horse Year of the sixty cycle (A.D. 1353), he dispatched Brag-dkar-ba shes-rab-bkra-shis to Beijing to offer to Thu-hun-thi-mur, the emperor of the Yuan Dynasty, many tributes including a lion's skin. The Yuan emperor appointed Byang-chub rgyal-mtshan to the official post of *da si-tu* (cabinet minister) and bestowed on him the diploma of hereditary rights to rule over Tibetan local regimes and a seal of authority. Brang-chub rgyal-mtshan established thirteen *rdzong* (equivalent to "county" in interior China); among them were Gzhis-kha-rtse-rdzong, Sne'u-rdzong, Gong-dkar-rdzong, Brag-dkar-rdzong, 'Phyong-rgyas-stag-rtse-rdzong, Gnyal-lhun-rtse-rdzong, Romg-rin-spung-rdzong, Kags-rtse-gri-gu-rdzong, and 'Ol-kha-stag-rtse-rdzong. He set up rules stipulating that the term of office of each *rdzong-dpon*, the head of a *rdzong*, was three years; and he worked out a set of laws called Fifteen Laws.*

---

*The ancient Fifteen Laws were: (1) praise of a brave man by covering his back with a tiger-skin, (2) denunciation of a coward by covering his back with a fox-skin, (3) the system of promoting and punishing local officials, (4) distinguishing of the true from the false when listening to appeals, (5) the process of arrest and summons for interrogation, (6) the way of extorting a confession by torture, (7) imposition of fines on law-breakers, (8) regulations regarding taxation, (9) death sentence for murderers, (10) punishment for people who wound others, (11) punishment for people who have perfidiously torn up agreements or contracts, (12) punishment for thieves, (13) marriage and divorce law, (14) punishment for people who commit adultery, (15) regulations regarding the borrowing or lending of money.

At about the same time that the high-ranking monks of the Phag-gru sect were seizing Tibetan administrative power, Zhu Yuanzhang, the first emperor of the Ming Dynasty, ascended the throne in the Earth Monkey year of the sixth cycle (A.D. 1368). In the Water Rat year of the sixth cycle of the Tibetan calendar (A.D. 1373), the Ming court set up in Tibet an administrative apparatus called the "Dbus-Gtsang Commandery," vested the clerical chiefs of the Phag-gru sect with government posts and administrative power, and thus strengthened the Tibetan local polity based on the merging of religious and secular rule and controlled by the clerical chiefs of the Phag-gru Bka'-brgyud sect. The Ming court's policy towards other Buddhist sects was to treat them equally and let them get along with one another peacefully. In the year when the Ming court established the Dbus-Gtsang Commandery, the fourth Living Buddha of the Karma Bka'-brgyud (Black Hat) sect Rol-pa'i rdo-rje sent his envoy to Nanjing to offer tributes to the Emperor Zhu Yuanzhang and express good wishes for the founding of the Ming Dynasty. All the emperors of the Ming court and the successive Living Buddhas of the Karma Bka'-brgyud sect had a very close relationship. The emperors granted the Living Buddhas various honorific titles such as "State Tutor," "King of Expounding Buddhism," and "Great Treasure King of Dharma." And the influence and power of the Karma Bka'-brgyud sect grew stronger and stronger with each passing day.

Later, 'Jam-dbyangs-gushri Shakya-rgyal-mtshan came into power for nine years beginning in the Wood Serpent year of the sixth cycle of the Tibetan calendar (A.D. 1365). In the ninth year of his reign, the year of the Water Rat (A.D. 1373), Zhu Yuanzhang, the founding emperor of the Ming Dynasty, granted him such titles as *da si-tu* (cabinet minister), *Qingguogong* (Duke of Qingguo), and "State Tutor of *Murddhabhichikta*," and bestowed on him an imperial diploma and a jade seal to authorize him to rule over Tibet with plenary power.

After him, Spyan-snga grags-pa byang-chub came into power for eight years beginning in the Water Ox year of the sixth cycle of the Tibetan calendar (A.D. 1373).

Then Spyan-snga bsod-nams grags-pa came into power for five years beginning in the Iron Cock year of the sixth cycle (A.D. 1381).

After his reign Grags-pa rgyal-mtshan came into power for forty-seven years beginning in the Wood Ox year of the sixth cycle of the Tibetan calendar (A.D. 1385). In the fourth year of his reign, the Earth Dragon year of the seventh cycle (A.D. 1388), he was given the title of "King" and a gold seal of authority. In the twenty-fifth year of his reign, or the Earth Ox year of the seventh cycle (A.D. 1409), he was granted the title of "King of Expounding Buddhism" and a jade seal of authority by the Ming Emperor Yong Le. It was in the same year that Tsong-kha-pa built Dga'-ldan Monastery as his residential quarter, and founded the Dge-lugs (Yellow) sect. At that time the patrons who contributed the land for building the monastery and paid all the expenditures for the construction were Grags-pa rgyal-mtshan, the King of Sne'u-rdzong; Nang-so rim-chen-lhum-po and Nang-so-rgya-po, the two brothers living at Brag-dkar-gzhis-ka; and Zla-ba, the chief of Rgya-ma *wan-hu*. They contributed large pieces of land and many manorial estates at Mal-gro-klung-shod. Tsong-kha-pa recruited many disciples from the Dbus-Gtsang, Mnga'-ris, Khams, and Qinghai regions. These people later returned to their homelands and built many monasteries, among which the most prestigious are the three main monasteries at Lhasa—the Se-ra Monastery, the 'Bras-spungs Monastery, and the Dga'-ldan Monastery—and the Bkra-shis-lhun-po Monastery at Gzhis-kha-rtse (Xigaze).

Eight years after the founding of the Dga"-ldan Monastery, or in the Fire Monkey year of the seventh cycle (A.D. 1416), Tsong-kha-pa's disciple 'Jam-dbyangs-chos-rgyal bkra-shi-dpal-ldan founded 'Bras-spungs Monastery. The patron who paid for the expenditures and donated manorial estates was Nam-mkha' bzang-po, the *rdzong-dpon* of Sne'u-rdzong.

Four years after the founding of the 'Bras-spungs Monastery, or in the Earth Pig year of the seventh cycle of the Tibetan calendar (A.D. 1419), Byams-chen-chos-rgyal Shakya ye-shes, another of Tsong-kha-pa's disciples, founded the Se-ra Monastery. The patrons who paid for the expenditures and donated the land for building were Nam-mkha' bzang-po, the *rdzong-dpon* of Sne'u-rdzong, and his son Nam-mkha dpal-'byor.

Twenty-eight years after the founding of the Se-ra Monastery, or in the Fire Hare year of the eighth cycle (A.D. 1447), Tsong-kha-pa's disciple Dge-'dun grub (the first Dalai Lama) founded Bkra-shis-lhun-po Monastery. The patron responsible for the expenditure and the land for building was Hor-dpal-'byor bzang-po, the then *rdzong-dpon* of Gzhis-kha-rtse. From then on, the Dge-lugs sect developed rapidly, gaining more and more influence and power, and this made it strong enough to compete with the Karma Bka'-brgyud sect as well as other Bka'-brgyud sects.

3. Internal Wars Among the Rulers of the Phag-gru Regime

After Grags-pa rgyal-mtshan, the *sde-si* (king) of the Phags-gru regime, died, Grags-pa byung-gnas came into power for thirteen years beginning in the Water Rat year of the seventh cycle of the Tibetan calendar (A.D. 1432). In the second year of his reign, *spyan-snga* (district governor) Bsod-nams rgyal-mtshan died, and Grags-pa byung-gnas's father Che-sa sangs-rgyas rgyal-mtshan attempted to seize the political power of Sne'u-gdong (in the Lha-kha region) by every possible means. This kindled the flames of conflict between father and son; the warfare lasted for many years and was called in Tibetan chronicles "Sde-si's crisis in the year of the Tiger" or "the civil war of Phag-gru-pa." Rin-spungs-pa Nor-pu bzang-po, one of the ministers under Grags-pa byung-gnas, took the opportunity provided by Phag-gru-pa's civil war and occupied Lhun-grub-rtse (Gzhis-kha-rtse) and some other *rdzong* and *chol kah* (districts) of the Gtsang region. From then on the Phag-gru-pa regime began to decline.* In the ninth year of Grags-pa byung-gnas's reign, or the Iron Monkey year of the seventh cycle (A.D. 1440), the Ming Emperor Ying Zong dispatched some envoys to Tibet to confer on Grags-pa bryung-gnas the title of "King," a diploma, and a seal of authority. He was called Dbang (king) Grags-pa byung-gnas.

Later, Dbang Kun-dga' legs-pa came into power for four years beginning in the Wood Ox year of the seventh cycle (A.D. 1445). Emperor Ying Zong of the Ming Dynasty bestowed on him the title of "King of Expounding Buddhism." Owing to his incompetence in political affairs and his family's failure to keep on good terms among themselves, Nor-pu bzang-po, the *rdzong-dpon* of Rin-spungs rdzong, and his son took advantage of the occasion and seized a greater part of power over the Gtsang region.

Later, Dbang Rin-chen rdo-rje came into power for seven years beginning in the Earth Dragon year of the eighth cycle (A.D. 1448). Emperor Ying Zong of the Ming Dynasty conferred the title of "King of Expounding Buddhism" on him.

At the time, Rin-spungs-pa Nor-pu bzang-po's second son

A Divine Key to the Royal Lineage says that there was nobody at the helm of the Phag-gru regime for three years. Some other annals say that Che-sa sangs-rgyas rgyal-mtshan gained sovereignty during this period. According to the *Religious History of Lho-rong*, written by Ri-bo-che dpon-tshang tshe-dbang-rgyal in the Fire Hare year of the eighth cycle (A.D. 1447), since Grags-pa byung-gnas failed to keep on good terms with Che-sa sangs-rgyas rgyal-mtshan, the latter lived at Ya-rgyab for a few years. He became a local official at Rtsed-thang (modern Zedang) afterwards, but he had never gained sovereignty. Such a statement is more reliable.

Kun-bzang-pa, third son Don-grub-rdo-rje and fourth son Mtsho-rgyal-rdo-rje, and Kun-bzang-pa's youngest son Don-yod-rdo-rje gradually occupied many *rdzong* and *chol-kha* of the Gtsang region, and this pushed the rulers of the Rin-spungs-pa sect into continuous warfare with the rulers of the Phag-gru-pa sect.

4. The War Between the Rin-spungs-pa and the Dge-lugs-pa

Spyan snga Ngag-gi dbang-po came into power for thirty-eight years beginning in the Wood Dog year of the eighth cycle* (A.D. 1454). Not long after his coming into reign, the ruling class failed to keep on good terms within itself, and once more a state of turmoil developed. In the Iron Ox year of the eighth cycle (A.D. 1481), Chos-grags-yes-shes of the Karma Bka'-brgyud (Red) sect incited Rin-spungs-pa Nor-pu bzang-po's son Kun-bzang-pa and the latter's son Don-yod-rdo-rje to lead ten thousand men of the Gtsang troops to attack the Dbus region. The *drzong-dpon* of Sne'u, *rdzong* Ngag-dbang-bsod-nams-lhum-po, and his son Ngag-dbang-bsod-nams-rnam-rgyal, the then patrons of the Dge-lugs sect, were compelled to flee.

In the Water Ox year of the eighth cycle (A.D. 1493), Emperor Xiao Zong of the Ming Dynasty conferred the title of "King" on *spyan snga* ngag-gi dbang-po, but *spyan snga* ngag-gi dbang-po died before the imperial envoy who was to give him the imperial diploma and gifts arrived in Tibet. His son Ngag-dbang-bkra-shis-grags-pa was too young to exercise control, so it was decided that before his coming of age, Chos-grags-yes-shes, the fourth Living Buddha of the Red Hat system, and Mtsho-rgyal-rdo-rje, Rin-spungs-pa Nor-pu bzang-po's son, should act for him. These two people exercised administrative

---

New Red Annals is wrong in saying that it was in the Iron Ox year of the eighth cycle.

authority for nine years. In the Earth Horse year of the eighth cycle (A.D. 1498), they were instigated by Tshul-khrims-rgya-mtsho, the seventh Living Buddha of the Karma-pa (Black Hat) sect to forbid the Dge-lugs monks of the Se-ra, 'Bras-spungs, and Dga'-ldan monasteries to take part in the Grand Prayer Meeting at Lhasa. During the following twenty years, the Lhasa Grand Prayer Meetings were attended only by the monks from the monasteries of the Bka'-brgyud sect and Sa-skya sect in the Lhasa area.

Later, Dbang Ngad-dbang bkra-shis grags-pa gained sovereignty and began to exercise power in the Earth Sheep year of the eighth cycle (A.D. 1499). In order to suppress the Se-ra, 'Bras-spungs, and Dga'-ldan monasteries, Rin-spungs-pa don'-yod-rdo-rje founded Thub-bstan-chos-khor-gling Monastery (generally called "the New Monastery of the Karma-pa") at Sa-nag to the east of Lhasa in the Water Pig year of the eighth cycle (A.D. 1503).

Thirteen years after Dbang Ngag-dbang bkra-shis grags-pa came into power, in the Water Monkey year (A.D. 1512), he was given the title of "King" by the Ming Emperor Wu Zong, and from then on became more influential. In the Earth Tiger year of the ninth cycle (A.D. 1518), he allowed the monks of the Se-ra, 'Bras-spungs, and Dga'-ldan monasteries to resume their right to take part in the Grand Prayer Meeting at Lhasa in the first month of the year, and he asked the second Dalai Lama Dge-'dun rgya-mtsho to preside over the Grand Prayer Meeting every year. In addition to this, he presented one of his mansion houses, called Rdo-khang-sngon-mo (blue stone house), to the Dalai Lama as a gift. This mansion was renamed Dga'-ldan-pho-brang. Later, when the fifth Dalai Lama gained the sovereignty of the Tibetan regime, Dga'-ldan-pho-brang became an alternative name for the Tibetan local government.

Later, in the Fire Dog year of the ninth cycle of the Tibetan calendar (A.D. 1526), Kun-dga' Rin-chen, the district governor of the Bri-gung-pa, instigated the troops stationed at Kong-po and Zhod-kha to capture Dga'-ldan Monastery's manorial estates in the areas controlled by the Bri-gung-pa sect. Thus, a war broke out between the Bri-gung-pa and the Dge-lugs-pa. The supporters of the Dge-lugs-pa were the *rdzong-dpon* of Sne'u-rdzong and *sde-srid* Skyid-shod-pa—two secular manorial lords.

In the Fire Cock year of the ninth cycle of the Tibetan calendar (A.D. 1537), when the second Dalai Lama Dge-'dun rgya-mtsho was residing at Chos-'Khor-rgyal, the troops of the Bri-gung-pa sect launched attacks from 'Od-kha and occupied eighteen Dge-lugs-pa monasteries and temples in the Bri-gung and Mal-gro areas, forcing their monks to convert to the Bri-gung sect and change the colour of their hats. For many years after this, at some places where the Bri-gung Bka'-brgyud sect predominated, the monks of the Dge-lugs-pa had to have two hats, wearing their yellow hats only in private.

5. The War Between *Sde-srid* Gtsang-pa and the Dge-lugs-pa

In the Wood Ox year of the ninth cycle of the Tibetan calendar (A.D. 1565), Emperor Shi Zong of the Ming Dynasty conferred on Ngag-dbang Bkra-shis grags-pa the titles of "King of Expounding Buddhism," "State Tutor of *Murddhabhichikta*," and "King of Dharma." At that time in Tibet in the upper part of lho-kha, *sde-srid** Yar-rgyab-pa was the strongest chief; in the lower part of the lho-kha, Dwags-po, Kong-po, Leh, Lo-ro, and Byar areas, *sde-srid* Sku-rab-pa was the strongest; in the Gtsang region, *sde-srid* Gtsang-pa was the strongest. They all were patrons of the Bka-'brgyud sect. In other places the strong chiefs included *sde-srid* Lha-rgya-ri and *sde-srid* Skyid-shod-pa,

---

* *Sde-srid* is an alternative name for *sde-pa*, the local chief of an area in ancient Tibet.

who reigned between the Lhasa River and the Mal-gro area; both of them were patrons of the Dge-lugs sect.

Sde-srid Shing-shag-pa Tshe-bstan-rdo-rje and Bri-gung-pa tried to unite their forces to destroy the Dge-lugs sect. For this purpose they decided that they should first of all destroy *sde-srid* Skyid-shod-pa, who supported the Dge-lugs-pa economically. So, in the Wood Serpent year of the tenth cycle (A.D. 1605), they mobilized the troops of the Gtsang region and those of the Zho-dkar and Zho-nag areas and defeated *sde-srid* Skyid-shod-pa, the patron of the Dge-lugs-pa, killing and wounding many opponents.

Although *sde-srid* Yar-rgyab-pa Bdud-'dul-grags-pa and *sde-srid* Gtsang-pa Phun-tshogs rnam-rgyal were relatives (Gtsang-pa Phuntshogs rnam-rgyal's wife was Yar-rgyab-pa's daughter; the wife of Phun-tshogs rnam-rgyal's brother Phun-tshogs-rin-'dzin was also Yar-rgyab-pa's daughter), they were not on good terms. In the Iron Dog year of the tenth cycle (A.D. 1610), *sde-srid* Gtsang-pa Phun-tshogs rnam-rgyal led his troops to attack Yar-rgyab-pa, who was captured and put into prison. In the Water Rat year of the tenth cycle (A.D. 1612) and the following year (the year of the Water Ox), Gtsang-pa-khan (an alternative name for *sde-srid* Gtsang-pa) Phun-tshogs rnam-rgyal once more precipitated a war and conquered Phan-po and Sne'u-rdzong. He seized the whole region of Gtsang and prohibited the search for the "soul boy" of the incarnation of the fourth Dalai Lama Yon-tan rgya-mtso. This is called in the Tibetan chronicles "the riot in the years of the Rat and Ox."

In order to cope with such a circumstance, *sde-srid* Skyid-shod-pa Bsod-nams-ram-rgyal, the patron of the Dge-lugs-pa, presented the statue of Bodhisattva Avolokitesvara of the Potala Palace as a gift to Chos-'Khor-khan and his brother, the chiefs of the Kharkha tribe of the Western Mongols, and asked them to attack *sde-srid* Gtsang-pa for the Dge-lugs-pa. In the Fire Serpent year of the tenth cycle (A.D. 1617)—the year when the fifth Dalai Lama was born—more than three thousand troops of the Kharkha Mongols under the command of Chos-'Khor-khan arrived in the Dubs region and together with the Dbus troops launched attacks on *sde-srid* Gtsang-pa. In the seventh month of the following year by the Tibetan calendar, *sde-srid* Gtsang-pa Phun-tshogs rnam-rgyal marched with more than ten thousand men into the Dbus region by way of Stod-lung, occupied the Se-ra and 'Bras-spungs monasteries, killed more than five thousand monks there, and forced the fourth Panchen Erdeni Blo-bzang chos-kyi rgyal-mtshan to flee to the Mnga'-ris region. All the remaining monks of the Se-ra and 'Bras-spungs monasteries planned to flee to Qinghai. When they arrived at Stag-lung Monastery on their journey, Zhabs-drung-ngag-dbang-rnam-rgyal, the abbot of Stag-lung Monastery, financed their stay at his monastery for four months and persuaded them not to go to Qinghai. At the same time he asked *sde-srid* Gtsang-pa to let them return to their own monasteries, and his request was granted. Later, in order to repay his kindness, the three main monasteries—Se-ra, 'Bras-spungs, and Dga'-ldan—decided to give Stag-lung Monastery all the tea left over from the Lhasa Grand Prayer Meeting in the first month of the Tibetan calendar every year, and to give every monk of the Stag-lung Monastery a share of the donations collected at the Grand Prayer Meeting.

The joint forces of the Dbus region and Mongols being defeated, the Mongol troops evacuated from Tibet; the Se-ra and the 'Bras-spung monasteries paid a large sum in fines to *sde-srid* Gtsang-pa. The fifth Dalai Lama's chief Butler Bsod-nams-rab-brtan, in order to seek his revenge on *sde-srid* Gtsang-pa, came to the latter's residence to ask permission to go to Chos-'khor-rgyal Monastery, saying that he had to fetch the last Dalai Lama's personal belongings. His request being granted, he made a pretence of going to Chos-'khor-rgyal Monastery by way of Mal-gro, but in reality he went to Qinghai by way of Kong-po and Nag-zhod to ask Gu-ru-hung-theci and his brother Blo-bzang-bstan-'dzim, the strongest Mongol force in Qinghai at that time, to dispatch troops to help the Dge-lugs sect.

Sde-srid Gtsang-pa Phun-tshogs-rnam-rgyal died of small-pox in the Iron Sheep year of the eleventh cycle of the Tibetan calendar (A.D. 1631). His son Karma-bstan-skyong-dbang-po came into power in the Water Monkey year of the eleventh cycle (A.D. 1632). He ordered that, except for the thirteen main strongholds such as Gzhis-kha-rtse, all the fortresses at places difficult of access and likely to be used by the rebels as bases be destroyed. He added a law about security in the border regions to the Fifteen Laws worked out by Phag-gru-pa and Tshal-pa Sde-srid, thus formulating the "Sixteen Laws." In addition, he worked out a unified Tibetan system of weights and measures which was generally called *Bstan-tshad-kha-ru* (meaning "legal standard").

In the following year, the Water Cock year of the eleventh cycle (A.D. 1633), the chief butler Bsod-nams-rab-brtan together with Mongol chieftains Lha-btsun-chung-ba and Blo-bzang-bstan-'dzin led a group of two thousand Mongol cavalrymen to the Dbus-Gtsang region and launched a counterattack together with *sde-srid* Skyid-shod-pa's troops of the Dbus region against *sde-srid* Gtsang-pa's troops. *Sde-srid* gtsang-pa's troops were defeated, and they tried to retreat to Rkyang-thang-sgang and Lcags-po-ri but were stopped by a river. The Mongol cavalry-men attacked the defeated troops and killed several thousand Tibetan soldiers. Before the Mongols launched their second attack, the fourth Panchen Blo-bzang chos-kyi rgyal-mtshan, *dga'-ldan-khi-pa* (highest abbot of the Yellow sect) Dkon-mchog-chos-'pher, and *stag-lung-zhabs-drung* (governor) Ngag-dbang-rnam-rgyal came to mediate between the two parties. They proposed an armistice agreement which stipulated that Dga'-ldan-pho-brang (palace of Dga'-ldan) enjoy the ownership of all the monasterial estates in Lhasa and to the south of the

Lhasa River; that the chief butler Bsod-nams-rab-brtan live in 'Bras-spungs-pho-brang; that *sde-srid* Gtsang-pa return all the manorial estates which he had seized from the Se-ra, 'Bras-spungs, and Dga'-ldan monasteries to their original owners; that all the Dge-lugs-pa monasteries in both the Dbus and Gtsang regions which had been converted to the Bka'-brgyud sect by force be restored to the Dge-lugs-pa sect; that Phan-po-khar-rtse-*rdzong* be handed over to *sde-srid* Skyid-shod-pa; and that *sde-srid* Gtsang-pa recognize the status of the soul boy of the fourth Dalai Lama. *Sde-srid* Gtsang-pa accepted all the terms except the last one. He refused to recognize the incarnate soul boy of the fourth Dalai Lama; by then the fifth Dalai Lama was only five years old. He refused to recognize the fourth Dalai Lama's right to reincarnate because he was afraid that the reincarnation of the fourth Dalai Lama Yon-tan rgya-mtsho might strengthen the economic power of the Dga'-ldan-pho-brang of the 'Bras-spungs Monastery and would do harm to the religious influence of the Karma Bka'-brgyud sect; and, in the long run, if the Dga'-ldan-pho-brang's political power became strong enough, it would ride roughshod over *sde-srid* Gtsang-pa himself.

6. Elimination of the *Sde-srid* Gtsang-pa Regime by Gu-shri Khan, Establishment of the Original Tibetan Local Government, and Suppression of the Rebellion of the Karma Bka'-brgyud Sect

After losing the war, *sde-srid* Gtsang-pa began to seek a strong political patron in order to revenge himself against the Dge-lugs sect. Ever since Liu Liu and Liu Qi had started a peasant uprising in the hinterland of our country in the Earth Serpent year of the ninth cycle of the Tibetan calendar (A.D. 1509), repeated peasant uprisings had broken out, which dealt heavy blows to the feudalist Ming court, severely weakened it, and pushed it to the verge of collapse. Lindan Khan,* the chieftain of eight Mongol tribes in Chahar, in the eighteenth year of his reign, or the Water Serpent year of the eleventh cycle of the Tibetan calendar (A.D. 1632), took the Qinghai area under his control and thus became very influential. At the same time in the Khams region, Don-yod rdo-rje, the local lord of Beri, captured Sde-dge, 'Dam-khor, Nay-shod-tsho-drug, Chab-mdo, and Ri-bo-che, also becoming very powerful. They both were Bon followers and were hostile to Buddhism, especially the Dge-lugs sect. So Gtsang-pa Khan Karma-bstan-skyong-dbang-po formed an alliance with these two people, vowing to destroy the three main monasteries of Se-ra, 'Bras-spungs, and Dga'-ldan and wipe out the Dge-lugs sect.

In the Wood Dog year of the eleventh cycle (A.D. 1634), Chahar Lindan Khan left Qinghai with his troops for Tibet to help Gtsang-pa Khan, but died accidentally on his way at Sha-ra-ta-la. In the same year the chieftain of the Kharkha tribe of the Mongols, Chos-thu Khan,** owing to internal conflicts with other tribes, was forced to leave Khob-do Kharkha with his tribe and moved to the Qinghai region. He and his followers conquered all the tribes in Qinghai, killed a great number of Dge-lugs monks, and put the rest into prison. At the same time, Don-yod rdo-rje, the local lord of Beri in the Khams region, destroyed most of the monasteries belonging to the Sa-skya, Dge-lugs, and Rnying-ma-pa sects and put the monks into jail.

When the news reached Lhasa that the Kharkha chieftain Chos-thu Khan was planning to march into Tibet, Bsod-nams chos-'pher, the chief butler of Dga'-ldan-pho-brang, and *sde-srid* Skyid-shod-pa Mtsho-ryal-rdo-rje dispatched several monks of

---

*Mongol prince Lindan Khan, a thirty-seventh generation descendant of the Mongol royal house, was ruler of the Chahar Mongols after the Yuan Dynasty was overthrown.

**A patron of the Bon religion.

the 'Bras-spungs Monastery to send a confidential letter to translators Sna-chen and Shani-cha-chen, asking them to go in disguise by way of Qinghai to meet with and ask help of Gu-shri Khan, the chieftain of the Dzungar Mongols.

In the following year, the Wood Pig year of the eleventh cycle (A.D. 1635), Chos-thu Khan, the Mongol chieftain of the Kharkha tribe, dispatched his son Ar-silan in command of several thousand troops to march into Tibet to support Gtsang-pa Khan. At the upper reaches of the Yangtze River, they met with Gu-shri Khan and Batur Huntheci, who, pretending to be merchants, were going to the Dbus and Gtsang regions to do a field survey. So they went to Lhasa together. Gu-shri-Khan persuaded Ar-silan not to do any harm to the Dge-lugs sect; consequently, when Ar-silan arrived at Lhasa, instead of supporting Gtsang-pa Khan, he led his troops to the Yar-'brog area to attack Gtsang-pa Khan's troops. In order to launch a counterattack, Gtsang-pa Khan gathered a great number of troops from north Gtsang to challenge Ar-silan. The Mongol troops retreated. While Ar-silan was at Lhasa, he had an interview with the fifth Dalai Lama and listened to his expounding of Buddhist sutras. This was reported by the Living Buddha of the Red Hat Karma Bka'-brgyud sect in a letter sent to Chos-thu Khan, Ar-silan's father, who was in Qinghai. Chos-thu Khan was very angry with his son because Ar-silan did not carry out his instructions, so he ordered that Ar-silan be killed. Not long after, Ar-silan was murdered by his subordinate Sde-che. Owing to this, Chos-thu Khan's plan of marching into Tibet to support Gtsang-pa Khan ended up with nothing definite.

Toward the end of autumn in the Fire Rat year of the eleventh cycle (A.D. 1636), Gu-shri Khan, once again pretending to be a merchant, together with Batur Huntheci and a few servants, arrived at Lhasa to make a survey of the situation in the Dbus and Gtsang regions. He had an interview with the fifth Dalai Lama and Panchen Lama, and the fifth Dalai Lama conferred on him the title of "King of Dharma, Protector of the Religion." Next year, with the help of Batur Huntheci, he led ten thousand troops to fight a battle with Chos-thu Khan's thirty thousand troops, and wiped them out in the end. Toward the end of that year, the whole tribe of Hoshod Mongols of which Gu-shri Khan was the chieftain moved from the Dzungar area into Qinghai and settled down there. Gu-shri Khan married his daughter Amindalan to Batur Huntheci's son, giving them rich and generous gifts. Then Batur Huntheci returned to the Dzungar area with his troops.

In the Earth Rat year of the eleventh cycle of the Tibetan calendar (A.D. 1639), Gu-shri Khan led his troops to attack the local lord of Beri, the supporter of Gtsang-pa Khan. After he had occupied Sde-dge and 'Bar-khams and wiped out the local lord of Beri, he sent Dge-bsnyen-dom-grub and Se-chen Wu-pa-shi as messengers to Lhasa to report the victory in the Khams region. The fifth Dalai Lama had said that he hoped Gu-shri Khan would return to Qinghai after defeating the local lord of Beri. He told his chief butler Bsod-nams chos-'pher on several occasions that it would be unwise to invite Gu-shri Khan's troops into Tibet to attack Gtsang-pa Khan. But Bsod-nams chos-'pher met the two messengers secretly at Dga'-ldan-khang-gsar (new residence) and asked them to take his confidential letter to Gu-shri Khan, in which he asked Gu-shri Khan to lead his troops into Tibet to attack Gtsang-pa Khan as he had attacked the local lord of Beri. After receiving the letter, Gu-shri Khan made a feint of retreating from 'Bar-Khans to Qinghai. When Gtsang-pa Khan relaxed his vigilance after being informed that Gu-shri Khan had retreated to Qinghai, Gu-shri Khan's troops suddenly appeared in the Dbus region and defeated Gtsang-pa Khan. At first the Mongols had no intention of killing the captured Gtsang-pa Khan Karma-bstan-skyong-dbang-po, but imprisoned him in an estate at Sne'u. But later, when searching Gtsang-pa Khan's cook Chos-dbyangs, they found in his clothes a document to the effect that the Red Hat and Black Hat Living Buddhas of the Karma Bka'-brgyud sect had formed an alliance with Gtsang-pa Khan, that they intended to destroy all the Dge-lugs monasteries including the three main monasteries, and that they would imprison the Panchen Lama and Dalai Lama at Kong-po. So the Gtsang-pa Khan was sealed into an ox-hide bag and drowned in the Yarlung Zangpo River not far from the Sne'u estate.

In the Water Horse year of the eleventh cycle of the Tibetan calendar (A.D. 1642), Gu-shri Khan, having gained sovereign power over the whole of Tibet, invitve the fifth Dalai Lama to Gzhis-kha-rtse (Xigaze). He handed over to the Dalai Lama the sovereign power over Tibet and innumerable treasures he had captured at Gtsang-pa Khan's palace in Ghis-kha-rtse. The original Tibetan government was thereby established. Later, the Bkra-shis-ri-lhun Monastery, newly built by Gtsang-pa Khan near the Bkra-shis-lhun-po Monastery, was pulled down, all its lumber was transported to Lhasa to replace the old lumber in the corridors of the Jokhang Temple, and most of its Buddha images and religious instruments were given to the Rnam-rgyal Grva-tshang (Theological College) in the Potala Palace. And most of the monasteries and temples which had been under Gtsang-pa-khan's patronage were converted to the Dge-lugs sect. Under such circumstances, Chos-dbyings-rdo-rje, the tenth Living Buddha of the Karma Bka'-brgyud (Black Hat) sect fled from Lhasa to the Lho-brag area.

At the end of the preceding year, the Phan-sde Monastery and other monasteries of the Bka'-brgyud Sect in the Kong-po area together with many tribal chieftains had precipitated a rebellion against the Dga'-ldan-pho-brang, occupied many places in the Gtsang and Lho-kha regions, and thus threatened the security of the Dga'-ldan-pho-brang. Bstan-'dzin Dalai Khan, Gu-shri Khan's son, led a Mongol-Tibetan joint force to Kong-po to suppress the rebellion. They destroyed many monasteries that belonged to the Karma Bka'-brgyud sect and forced its followers to convert to the Dge-lugs sect. All the monks of the Karma Bka'-brgyud sect had their hands marked and were assigned to be kept in the Dge-lugs sect monasteries. Under such severe suppression, Chos-dbyings-rdo-rje, the tenth Living Buddha of the Black Hat Karma Bka'-brgyud sect, fled from the Lho-brag area by way of Kong-po to seek the patronage of the local lord Mu of the Naxi nationality in Yunnan. After Gu-shri Khan and Bsod-nams chos-'pher, the chief butler of the fifth Dalai Lama, had dealt the devastating blow to the Gtsang-pa Khan regime and its supporters—the monasteries of the Karma Bka'-brgyud sect—the struggle between the Karma Bka'-brgyud sect and the Dge-lugs sect was brought to an end on the whole. Although the Karma Bka'-brgyud sect was seriously weakened by the military suppression, it still precipitated several rebellions afterwards, greatly threatening the security of the newly established Tibetan local government.

Under the circumstances, the local government had to find a strong and powerful political force as its patron, lest it should be overthrown by its enemies. By this time, in other parts of China, the repeated peasant uprisings had dealt crushing blows to and overthrown the Ming Dynasty, but the fruits of victory had been seized by the Manchu Emperor Shun Zhi, who founded the Qing Dynasty at Shenyang in northeast China in the Wood Monkey year of the eleventh cycle (A.D. 1644). Since the Qing Dynasty was strong, the fifth Dalai Lama and the fourth Panchen Blo-bzang chos-kyi rgyal-mtshan entrusted Se-chen-chos-rgyal to forward their letters and gifts to the newly founded Qing government, congratulating it and asking for its support.

At that time, the Qing government, being at the first stage of expansion of its political influence, in order to consolidate its sovereignty and to control Mongol and other national minority areas in China, needed the support of a religious sect which enjoyed high political and religious prestige and influence. The Qing government deemed it necessary to make use of the Dalai Lama and the Panchen Lama. Therefore Emperor Shun Zhi not only wrote letters in reply and sent his kind regards to the fifth Dalai Lama and the fourth Panchen Lama, but also invited the fifth Dalai Lama to come to Beijing to have a meeting with him in the Water Dragon year of the eleventh cycle (A.D. 1652). The emperor gave the Dalai Lama a grand welcome and bestowed on him a gilt album and a gold seal of authority. The album consisted of fifteen golden sheets, each of which was as thick as a piece of Tibetan paper, four fingers in width and one span in length; on them were inscribed in three languages—Han, Mongol, and Tibetan—the following words: "Rgya-mtsho Lama, Overseer of the Buddhist Faith on Earth Under the Great Benevolent Self-Subsisting Buddha of West Heaven, All-Knowing Bearer of the Thunderbolt." And on the gold seal were inscribed in four languages: "Dalai Lama, Overseer of the Buddhist Faith on Earth Under the Great Benevolent Self-Subsisting Buddha of West Heaven." Henceforth the power of the Tibetan local government headed by the Dalai Lama was greatly increased. The local government was a politico-religious regime controlled by the Dge-lugs sect, and it had relatively complete administrative and legal systems. The first *sde-srid* of the Tibetan local government was Bsod-nams-rab-brtan (also called Bsod-nams-chos-'pher). He declared a new "Thirteen Laws" by cancelling the first two and the last items of Gtsang-pa Khan's Sixteen Laws (the first being the law of rewarding a brave man by covering his back with a tiger skin; the second being the law of disgracing a coward by hanging a fox skin on his back; and the sixteenth having to do with the security of the border region), and his explanations of the remaining thirteen laws were different from the ones given before. He not only maintained the thirteen official posts inaugurated by the Sa-skya sect when it controlled the Tibetan local regime, but also inaugurated a number of new official posts,* such as *bka'-blon* (cabinet minister), *mda'-dpon* (military officer in command of five hundred men), *khrims-dpon* (judge), *bso-rigs-do-dom-pa* (administrator in charge of handicrafts), *rtsis-dpon* (director of the auditorial department), *gnyer-tshang* (official in charge of a storehouse), *mi-dpon* (administrative officer of Lhasa city), *rtswa-gnyer* (official in charge of fodder), *shing-gnyer* (official in charge of firewood), *tshong-dpon* (official in charge of commercial affairs), *gser-yig-pa* (messenger of the royal house), *yong-sdud-pa* (local government's rent-collector), *bkar-'jug-pa* (official in charge of reserve supply), *rdzong-dpon* (district governor), and *gzhis-sdod* (manager of a manorial estate).

At the same time he established a number of administrative institutions, such as *bka'-blon-shag (former Tibetan local government)*, *rtsis-khang* (institution in charge of finance), *zhol-pa-las-khung* (administrative organ in charge of the service of the Potala Palace), *zhib-khang-las-khung* (institution in charge of criminal cases), *snang-rtse-shag-las-khung* (judicial department), *rtse-'phral-bde-las-khung* (organ in charge of Dalai Lama's money and property), *shol-bla-brang phyag-mdzod-las-khung* (organ in charge of practising usury and paying religious expenditures), *lha-sa-gnyer-tshang-las-khung* (institution in charge of storehouses in Lhasa) *rtswa-gnyer-las-khung* (organ in charge of fodder), and *rtsam-bzhes-las-khung* (organ in charge of barley-cakes).

By this time, a number of clerical and lay officials were sent to Dar-rtse-mdo and other places east of the Jinsha River in the Khams region to take a population census, measure arable land, and register households. They compiled fifty-six register books listing the names of every *rdzong* and manor, their products, and taxation. The register books were stamped with the Dalai La-

---

*The secretariat of the local government (*bka'-shag, yig-tshang*) and many other institutions were established later during the reigns of the seventh, eighth, thirteenth, and fourteenth Dalai Lamas.

ma's seal. The fifth Dalai Lama, using his political power, built thirteen monasteries for all religious sects except the Bka'-brgyud sect, converted a part of Bka'-brgyud-pa's monasteries to the Dge-lugs sect, stipulated the number of monks in various monasteries and the monk corvée system, gave the three main monasteries—Se-ra, 'Bras-spungs, and Dga'-ldan—the right to manage their own manors and the people on them, and stipulated the amount of crops and money the government provided for the monasteries. The details of the stipulations can be found in *The Yellow Glaze* written by *sde-srid* Sangs-rgyas rgya-mtsho. Some data from the book are listed in the accompanying tables.

Number of Monasteries, Monks, and Nuns

Time	Place	Religious Sect	Number of Monasteries	Number of Monks
Wood Dog year of the 12th cycle (A.D.1694)	Dbus and north of Gtsang	All sects included	Total: 1,807	Total: 97,538
Earth Tiger year of the 12th cycle (A.D. 1698)	Dbus and north of Gtsang	Dge-lugs sect	Lamaseries 95 Nunneries 9 Total: 104	Monks 12,289 Nuns 447 Total: 12,736
"	Gtsang		Lamaseries 94 Nunneries 16 Total: 110	Monks 1,981 Nuns 423 Total: 2,404
"	Mnga'-ris		Lamaseries 34 Nunneries 0 Total: 34	Monks 1,785 Nuns 0 Total: 1,785
"	'Ol-kha, Dwags-po		Lamaseries 80 Nunneries 7 Total: 87	Monks 2,475 Nuns 356 Total: 2,831
"	E		Lamaseries 28 Nunneries 0 Total: 28	Monks 1,989 Nuns 0 Total: 1,989

		Lamaseries 24	Monks 2,723
,,	Lho-kha	Nunneries 0	Nuns 0
		Total: 24	Total: 2,723
,,	Kong-po	Lamaseries 23	Monks 7,177
		Nunneries 4	Nuns 235
		Total: 27	Total: 7,412
,,	Bar-khams	Lamaseries 38	Monks 1,370
		Nunneries 0	Nuns 0
		Total: 38	Total: 1,370
,,	Totals	Lamaseries 416	Monks 31,789
		Nunneries 36	Nuns 1,461
		Total: 452	Total: 33,250

Population in the 34 Dge-lugs-pa Monasteries and Their Manors During the Reign of the Fifth Dalai Lama

Name of Monastery	Number of Monks	Number of Lay Households	Annual Output of Grain Crop (*khal*)
'Bras-spungs	4,200	553	37,922
Se-ra	2,850	86	7,200
Chos-'khor-rgyal	471	216	6,750
Rnam-rgyal Gwra-tshang	180	240	18,562
Bkra-shis-lhun-po	2,500	50	2,600
Ri-bo-dbe-chen	500	10	1,062
Rwa-stod	300	17	1,500
Pha-bong-kha	16	13	660
Brag-dbar	147	16	600
Byang-chub	110	25	1,500
Byang-bsam-gtan-rtse	90	3	350
Bam-ring Chos-sde	200	10	1,100
Gangs-can-chos-'pher	350	17	1,400
Dbe	200	13	550
Lhun-rtse-chos-sde	196	59	4,200
Shel-dge-chos-sde	250	5	100
Dpal-'khor-chos-sde	746	8	550
Ri-bo-chos-gling	130	28	310

Chu-shul-thar-pa	127	30	200
'Phyos-bkra-shis-bde-chen	130	4	600
Dpa'-shod bsam-grub	300	815	2,730
De-mo-chos-rdzong	240	360	600
Rngod-a-rig-thang	130	6	1,600
Sho-pa-mdobshad-grub-gling	300	50	250
Yer-pa-gsang-sngags-gling	160	43	3,820
Rsyang-ro-gser-sding	70	40	1,740
Rgyal-lha-khang	130	15	1,327
Chag-nag	370	70	1,446
Lcam-mda'	320	160	1,360
Gnas-chung	101	77	4,048
Rwa-sgreng	131	n.a.	449
Rtse-tshogs-pa	50	13	3,055
Ri-chos-thub-bstan-dar-rgyas	150	143	7,464
Gtsug-nor-bu-dgon	100	56	1,751
Total	16,245	3,251	119,356

Number of Monasteries, Monks, and Lay Households Under the Jurisdiction of the Dalai Lama and Panchen Erdeni in the Water Ox Year of the Twelfth Cycle (A.D. 1733)

Jurisdiction	Monasteries	Monks	Lay Households
Dalai Lama	3,150	342,560	121,440
Panchen Lama	327	13,670	6,750

Total Number of Monasteries and Monks of All Religious Sects in the Wood Dog Year (A.D. 1694)

Regions	Monasteries	Monks
Dbus, Gtsang, Khams, Mnga'-ris, Lho-kha, Dwags-po, Kong-po.	1,807	97,528

Increase in Monasteries, Monks, and Lay Households During the Forty Years from the Wood Dog Year of the Twelfth Cycle (A.D. 1694) to the Water Ox Year of the Twelfth Cycle (A.D. 1733)

Monasteries Increased	Monks Increased	Lay Households Increased
1,777	221,742	Remains to be verified

Having controlled the local regime of Tibet, the fifth Dalai Lama not only gave many prestigious monasteries the power of managing their own manors and their subjects, but also gave them the privilege of independent judicial power. Some monasteries had no manors and subjects, so they had no judicial power, but they were provided with grain, tea, butter, etc., by the local government annually. The monasteries which occupied manors and had subjects were very strong economically and enjoyed great political influence; they were also exempt from corvée and taxes levied by the local government. But the subjects and serfs attached to the monasteries had to pay corvée and taxes to their manorial lords—the monasteries, the government, and the serfowners—just as the common people and serfs did to their own manorial lords. It can be seen that the more complete the politico-religious system was, the greater the misery the labouring people suffered under the exploitation of the three kinds of manorial lords.

Under the politico-religious administrative system, the monasteries which possessed manors and subjects acquired judicial power on clerical as well as civil affairs. Thus monasteries, which were supposed to be places for religious activities, acquired the characteristics of judicial departments. Punishment was imposed not only on serfs and slaves, but also on monks, and the punishment was not measured out according to Buddhist commandments, but according to the local government's law. Thus the system of punishment by Buddhist commandments became only a myth in historical stories.

The monasteries which enjoyed independent judicial power and privileges invested by the local government levied various corvée and taxes on serfs under their jurisdiction and exercised laws just as the feudal government did. This system was contrary to the Buddhist doctrines and theories. It put the monks in a position of not being able to maintain their original economic status and not being able to uphold the Buddhist canon. The high-ranking personnel of all sects served a dual purpose: they were at the same time monks engaging in religious activities and officials having political power in their hands. The broad masses of the people called them *bla-dpon* (meaning "monk official," "lama official") to show their respect to them, but this term itself had profound satiric implication.

During the reign of the fifth Dalai Lama his policy with regard to all other religious sects except the defeated Karma Bka'-brgyud sect was to unite with and neutralize them. This was of great benefit to the development of his sect's political power. But soon after his death, his successor made sectarian mistakes in his policy toward other religious sects, so conflicts flared again among the various groups.

7. The Contradictions Between the Rnying-ma-pa and the Dge-lugs-pa, and How the Upper Strata Elements Used Those Contradictions to Launch Wars for Political Power

The successive *sde-srid* (administrative governors) appointed by the fifth Dalai Lama at different times during his reign renovated and built many Dge-lugs-pa monasteries and converted most of the Karma Bka'-brgyud-pa monasteries to Dge-lugs-pa monasteries. They bestowed on Dge-lugs-pa and Rnying-ma-pa monasteries many manors and numerous serfs. The Dge-lugs-pa monasteries occupied the strongest position economically and politically among all religious sects. As the fifth Dalai Lama treated the Sa-skya, Rnying-ma-pa, and Dge-lugs-pa sects equally and without discrimination, so he commanded deep love and reverence among the lamas and *dge-bshes* of all monasteries who had no religious prejudices. Although some people who were biased against the Dge-lugs-pa did not pay him much respect, the majority of the people had great faith in him. Some books say that he mixed all the religious sects up, but that is not true. The authors of those books were obviously biased in favour of their own religious sect.

The fourth Panchen Blo-bzang chos-kyi rgyal-mtshan was also an eminent scholar at the time. He enjoyed great prestige in Dbus, Gtsang, Qinghai, Mongolia, Bhutan, and India. He scrupulously abided by the Dge-lugs-pa doctrines and never held other religious sects in contempt but was adept in establishing good relationships with them. The farsighted policy in political and religious affairs adopted by the fifth Dalai Lama and the fourth Panchen had a good effect on the unity of various religious sects and among the Tibetan people. All the monks of the Dge-lugs-pa held these two lamas in great esteem and looked upon them as incarnations of the supreme teacher Tsong-kha-pa. After the fourth Panchen died, the fifth Panchen Blo-bzang ye-shes was also held in great esteem by the monks. After the fifth Dalai Lama died, *sde-srid* Sangs-rgyas rgya-mtsho bestowed upon the Three Great Monasteries of Se-ra, 'Bras-spungs, and Dga'-ldan many manors and serfs, giving them energetic economic support. But, as he was a believer in the Rnying-ma sect, so in the Three Great Monasteries he commanded love and respect only among the monks who had no sectarian prejudice, while the ones who were biased toward the Dge-lugs sect did not like him, but were afraid of him.

Lhabzang Khan, grandson of Tibet's previous administrative ruler Gu-shri Khan,* was a follower of the Dge-lugs-pa. His religious tutors were the fifth Panchen Blo-bzang ye-shes and the first 'Jam-dbyangs Living Buddha Ngag-dbang-brtson-'grus. So, when Lhabzang Khan waged a war against *sde-srid* Sangs-rgyas rgya-mtsho for administrative power, the Three Great Monasteries came out to mediate between them and reached an agreement to the effect that *sde-srid* Sangs-rgyas rgya-mtsho should resign from his office of *sde-srid* and hand over his administrative power to Lhabzang Khan.

Later, Lhabzang Khan made a feint of returning to Qinghai, but in reality he gathered his forces in the Nagchu region. They advanced toward Lhasa along three routes—one army under the command of Lhabzang Khan himself by way of Dga'-mo Pass, the second under the command of Thu-gus-ja'-sang moving across Phan-po-sgo-la Mountain, and the third under the command of Rgyal-mo-tshe-ring-bkra-shis, Lhabzang Khan's wife, starting at Stod-lung. They captured Lhasa and eliminated the troops that *sde-srid* Sangs-rgyas rgya-mtsho had recruited from the thirteen *wan-hu* in the Dbus-Gtsang region. *Sde-srid* Sangs-rgyas rgya-mtsho fled from Lhasa to Gong-dka on an ox-hide raft; then he went to Stod-lung valley, planning to offer his surrender to Rgyal-mo-tshe-ring-bkra-shis on the condition that the sixth Dalai Lama Tshangs-dbyangs rgya-mtsho would guarantee his life. The answer was that the *mkhan-po* (abbots) of the Se-ra, 'Bras-spungs, and Dga'-ldan monasteries would come to meet him. But when the *mkhan-po* of the Three Great Monasteries were arriving, Rgyal-mo-tshe-ring-bkra-shis had *sde-srid* Sangs-rgyas rgya-mtsho arrested and executed immediately. It was a great irony that *sde-srid* Sangs-rgyas rgya-mtsho, who had made great contributions to the political and cultural developments of Tibet, should have been

---

*Lhabzang Khan's father was Bstan-'dzin Dalai Khan, the eldest son of Gu-shri Khan.

killed under the influence of religious prejudice.

During the thirteen years after *sde-srid* Sangs-rgyas rgya-mtsho had been killed, Lhabzang Khan became the ruler of the Tibetan local regime. In the second year of his reign, or the Fire Dog year of the twelfth cycle of the Tibetan calendar (A.D. 1705), he reported to Emperor Kang Xi that the sixth Dalai Lama Tshangs-dbyangs rgya-mtsho led an unconventional and unrestrained life, violated Buddhist law and discipline, and thus could not be the incarnation of the fifth Dalai Lama. The emperor dispatched a special envoy Pad-ma-bi-ca-chi to Tibet, dethroned the sixth Dalai Lama Tshangs-dbyangs rgya-mtsho, and sent him to the hinterland of China under escort. Later, Ye-shes rgya-mtsho, a beggar's newborn baby, was chosen as the incarnation of the fifth Dalai Lama and was enthroned in Potala Palace.

Not long after this, Lhabzang Khan's eldest son Dga'-ldan-ldan-dzin insisted on marrying Tshe-dbang rab-brtan's daughter, and Lhabzang Khan gave his consent at last, although reluctantly. Tshe-dbang rab-brtan, the chieftain of the Dzungar Mongols, had long dreamed of seizing Tibet's regime, so he planned to march into Tibet under the pretence of escorting his daughter, and to overthrow Lhabzang Khan. He sent a large number of troops to escort his daughter to Tibet, but at the same time he dispatched his main forces to the Mnga'-ris region from where they marched eastward. These two groups of about 6,000 calvarymen joined forces in the vicinity of 'Dam-gzhung.

Although Lhabzang Khan had sensed that Tshe-dbang rab-brtan was evil-minded, he was not prepared for emergencies and could not launch an effective counterattack. The Dzungars adopted two devices to win over the Tibetan people. One was to give large handouts to the peasants and herders on their journey. The other was to conduct propaganda on a large scale to the effect that their purpose in marching into Tibet was not to gain their own benefit, but to salvage the Dge-lugs-pa's religious belief; they were going to invite the soul boy regarded as the incarnation of the Dalai Lama to Tibet—he had been born at Litang and at that time was living at Sku-'bum Monastery in Qinghai. Their propaganda spread far and wide, confused the Tibetans, and weakened their fighting spirit against the Dzungars. After the Dzungars had taken advantage of the favourable situation and defeated Lhabzang Khan's troops, Lhabzang Khan himself and one of his servants ran out of Potala Palace and fought desperately with a dozen Dzungars. They killed most of them but were themselves killed in the end. This happened in the Fire Cock year of the twelfth cycle of the Tibetan calndar (A.D. 1717).

From then on, the Dzungars ruled over Tibet for three years. Although they appointed the seventy-odd-year-old Lha-rgyal rab-brtan to be the *sde-srid* of Tibet, in reality all power was controlled by the Dzungars. Many Rnying-ma-pa monasteries were destroyed, including the historically well-known Rdo-rje-brag Monastery (the main monastery of the North transmission Rnying-ma-pa sect, in modern Zarang County) and the Smin-drug Monastery (the main monastery of the South transmission Rnying-ma-pa sect, also in modern Zarang County). Many eminent Rnying-ma-pa lamas were killed, including Pad-ma 'Phrin-las, the Living Buddha of the Rdo-rje-brag Monastery; Pad-ma-'gyur-med-rgya-mtsho, the abbot of the Smin-drug Monastery; and the famous Buddhist sutra translator Darmashri. When the Dzungars tried to destroy the fifth Dalai Lama's golden stupa, which was decorated with rare treasures and jewellery and was famed as "a wonder of the South Djambugling (one of the four continents of the Buddhist universe)," *sde-srid* Lha-rgyal rab-brtan stopped them with all his tactics.

When Tshe-dbang rab-brtan led his Dzungar troops into Tibet, buying popular support with material benefits and proclaiming that they were the protectors of the soul boy, they deceived the upper strata elements, religious circles, and broad masses of the Tibetan society. By flaunting the banner of religion and nation, the Dzungars usurped the Tibetan regime. This was a tragedy in the history of Tibet.

8. The Decline of the Politico-Religious System and the Internal Struggle for Power Within the Ruling Class

At this time in Qinghai, Dga'-ldan-er-de-spyi-nong, an official of noble Mongol origin, and Prince Blo-bzang bstan-'dzin escorted Bskal-bzang rgya-mtsho, the soul boy born at Litang and regarded as the incarnation of the Dalai Lama, from Litang to Qinghai by way of Sde-dge, and they made a report about this to Emperor Kang Xi. The emperor issued an edict to approve and confirm the status of Bskal-bzang rgyal-mtsho as the incarnation of the sixth Dalai Lama and permitted him to go to Tibet, so the seventh Dalai Lama Bskal-bzang rgya-mtsho was enthroned in Potala Palace in the Iron Ox year of the twelfth cycle (A.D. 1721).

After one year of the reign of a council consisting of the Han and Tibetan officials General Da'i-si, Lord Tshe-dbang nor-bu, King of Don-grub, Prince Blo-bzang bstan-'dzin, Nga-phod rdo-rje rgyal-po, and Lum-pa-nas bkra-shis rgyal-po, Emperor Kang Xi dispatched Asakhan, an imperial envoy, to Tibet. He appointed Khang-chen-nas the chief *bka'-blon*, with Nga-phod rdo-rje rgyal-po and Lum-pa-nas bkra-shis rgyal-po as his assistants. And then he appointed Pho-lha-nas and Sbyar-ra-nas as *bka'-blon* and conferred on them the title of *the-ci*. Among these *Bka'-blon*, Khan-chen-nas advocated only the Dge-lugs-pa, but had a dislike for other religious sects, especially the Rnying-ma-pa; while Nga-phod, Lum-pa-nas, and Sbyar-ra-nas advocated only the Rnying-ma-pa, but had a dislike for other religious sects. Pho-lha-nas was an adherent of Rnying-ma-pa, but outwardly pretended that he followed Dge-lugs-pa.

In the Water Hare year of the twelfth cycle of the Tibetan calendar (A.D. 1723), Emperor Yong Zheng dispatched Bande-mdor-mkhar, an imperial envoy, to Tibet with an imperial decree to the effect that the Dalai Lama should study and master all the important Buddhist sutras and agama (doctrinal method), that the Rdo-rje-brag Monastery, Smin-drug Monastery, and other monasteries which had been destroyed by the Dzungar Mongols were not to be restored, that the Yellow Hat (Dge-lugs-pa) sect should be further developed, that *bka'-blon* should go to Beijing to have an interview with the emperor, that the Dalai Lama's father should not interfere in political affairs, that all the *bka'-blon* should unite as one and improve government affairs, and so on. So, Khang-chen-nas decided to transfer the monks of the Rnam-rgyas gwra-tshang of Potala Palace to Dbu-can-dgon Monastery at Rtsed-thang, because they all were Rnying-ma-pa monks, and to transfer some of the monks from the Esoteric College to reorganize the Rnam-rgyas gwra-tshang; and he decided that all the Rnying-ma-pa monasteries which had been destroyed by the Dzungars were not to be renovated. His decision made other *bka'-blon*, especially Nga-phod, Lum-pa-nas, and Sbyar-ra-nas, nurse a grievance against him. The three of them therefore conspired to eliminate both Khang-chen-nas and Pho-lha-nas. When their plot became known to Mdo-mkhar-zhabs-drung tshe-ring-dbang-rgyal, he secretly informed Pho-lha-nas with a message hidden in a string of beads. Pho-lha-nas informed Khang-chen-nas about the critical situation and asked him to be prepared for all emergencies. But the latter did not believe Pho-lha-nas's words, and so did not enhance his vigilance.

Under the circumstances, Pho-lha-nas found an excuse and went back to his manor. A few days later, Nga-phod, Lum-pa-nas, and Sbyar-ra-nas launched a surprise attack and killed Khang-chen-nas in the grand chanting-sutra hall upstairs in the entrance building of Jokhang Temple, and on the same day they

83

killed Khang-chen-nas, his two wives and their children and all their servants at Dpal-'byor-rab-brtan, at the top of Jokhang Temple. At the same time, they dispatched Drung-'khor skyid-pa-thang-pa with 300 troops to the Gtsang region to arrest Pho-lha-nas, but they failed because he had fled to the Mnga'-ris region. Pho-lha-nas allied himself with Nor-yam, Khang-chen-nas's elder brother, and led the Gtsang troops and inflicted a crushing defeat on Nga-phod, Lum-pa-nas, and Sbyar-ra-nas. There is an account in detail of this incident in *The Biography of Pho-lha-nas*. The essence of the contradictions between Khang-chen-nas and Pho-lha-nas on the one hand and Bka'-blons Nga-phod, Lum-pa-nas, and Sbyar-ra-nas on the other hand was the struggle to seize political power. But they concealed the true purpose of their struggle and made the public believe that they differed in policy toward various religious sects. This caused serious confrontation between residents in the Dbus region and those in the Gtsang region and gave rise to a war between them. It is clear from the foregoing account that prejudice and enmity harboured by the various sects were detrimental to the Tibetan people and, furthermore, were used by the ruling class in their struggle for power.

During the period from the death of the fifth Dalai Lama to the reign of 'Gyur-med rnam-rgyal, Pho-lha-nas's son, the sixth Dalai Lama Tshangs-dbyangs rgya-mtsho and the seventh Dalai Lama Bskal-bzang rgya-mtsho, being under age, could exercise religious power only, while the political power was controlled by the successive *sde-srids* of the local government. When 'Gyur-med rnam-rgyal came into power, he did not pay much respect to the *amban*, the Qing imperial representatives in Tibet, whose offices were in Lhasa. He colluded with the Dzungar chieftain A-rgya-tshe-dbang rnam-rgyal rdo-rje and, furthermore, seriously threatened the seventh Dalai Lama's position and security. So, in the Iron Horse year of the thirteenth cycle of the Tibetan calendar (A.D. 1750) Fu Ching and

Rab-brtan, the two *amban*, sent a secret report to the emperor to the effect that 'Gyur-med rnam-rgyal was engaged in conspiratorial activities. The emperor decreed that troops under the command of an imperial envoy should be dispatched to Tibet to settle the question; but before their arrival in Tibet, special security measures should be taken and the *amban* should not be overanxious for a quick result. But the situation in Tibet soon became very serious. In the Iron Horse year of the thirteenth cycle (A.D. 1750), before the imperial envoy and troops arrived at Lhasa, *amban* Fu Ching and Rab-brtan, pretending to give a banquet in 'Gyur-med rnam-rgyal's honour at Khrom-gzigs-sgang (*amban*'s governmental office), suddenly had him arrested and summarily executed. Later, Blo-bzang bkra-shis, one of 'Gyur-med rnam-rgyal's die-hard followers, and a group of gangsters precipitated a rebellion and killed the two *amban*, all their subordinate officials and servants, and all the merchants of the Han nationality in the marketplace. They nearly eliminated all the Han residents in Lhasa. The seventh Dalai Lama Bskal-bzang rgya-mtsho and the assistant *bka'-blon* Mgon-po dngos-grub rab-brtan were at that time at Beijing. They submitted a report to Emperor Qian Long and suggested that a prestigious and influential imperial envoy be dispatched this time to Tibet; otherwise the leading members of the Tibetan administration might once again scramble for power and profit and launch a rebellion for their self-interest just as they had done before. So Emperor Qian Long thought it necessary to stipulate that all the administrative affairs should be managed by the two *amban* and he issued an edict on the matter.

When religious tutor Lcang-skya rol-pa'i rdo-rje heard about the edict, he stood up and said: "I dare not oppose Your Majesty's order. Although the two *amban* are capable of managing political affairs, yet they are not good at religious affairs. So, if Your Majesty invest all the administrative power on the two *amban* as your decree stated, I'm afraid that the religious position and influence of the Dalai Lama, Panchen Lama, and the Three Great Monasteries might be greatly weakened. Your Majesty resides in Beijing, while the two *amban* reside in Tibet. Your Majesty knows the situation in Tibet only from their reports, but they could make reports arbitrarily, so Your Majesty is not in a position to know what is actually happening in the Tibetan areas. So, if the *amban* were invested with all the administrative power to rule over Tibet and they did whatever they liked, the people in Tibet surely would nurse a grievance against Your Majesty. In order that the people in Tibet may maintain their faith and love in the Dalai Lama, Panchen Lama, and Your Majesty, please countermand the edict which has been issued. Only by this, may the future of Tibet and Central China be benefited and the Tibetan political and religious affairs be benefited. I am only a humble Tibetan monk under your patronage. However, it is my duty to serve Your Majesty and the State, so I ventured to state my views." The emperor turned his words in his mind again and again, and then said: "What Lcang-skya Huthugthu (meaning "the Living Buddha") said is really for the benefit of State affairs. I am determined to countermand the edict which has been issued and authorize the Dalai Lama to take charge of the administration of Tibet, and I'll appoint an *amban* to assist him. All the important issues in Tibet should be jointly decided by the Dalai Lama and the *amban*. I'll appoint four *bka'-blon* to work under the Dalai Lama, one of whom will be selected from the Dalai's attendant monk-officials. Will that do?" Lcang-skya Huthugthu saluted the emperor and said: "We are grateful for your benevolence and kindness." Later, the emperor decreed an edict on the basis of the above-mentioned principles.

In the Iron Sheep year of the thirteenth cycle of the Tibetan calendar, the sixteenth year of the reign of Emperor Qian Long (A.D. 1751), the Imperial Envoy Ban-de-mdor-mkhar arrived in Tibet. Bka'-shag (Kashag), the Tibetan local government, was officially founded for the first time, and the Thirteen-Article Ordinance for the More Efficient Governing of Tibet was worked out. These measures taken by the Qing court strengthened the rule of the Tibetan feudalist politico-religious system headed by the Dalai Lama.

In the newly established Bka'-shag, the Qing Dynasty emperor appointed one of the Dalai Lama's attendant monk-officials a Bka'-blon, who was not only the Dalai Lama's representative in the Bka'-shag but also the representative of all the monasteries. Thus the Bka'-shag became the supreme administrative institution—a merger of clerical and secular rule. From then on, the *mkhan-po* (abbots) and *spyi-gso* (chiefs of the finance departments of the Se-ra, 'Bras-spungs, and Dga'-ldan monasteries) began to take part in the enlarged conferences of the Bka'-shag. After the death of the seventh Dalai Lama, the office of regent was first set up. From then on, during the succeeding generations, before the time came for a new Dalai Lama to control the administrative power personally, the regent controlled the supreme administrative power. However, the Dalai or the regent could not make decisions on important questions by himself, but had to consult with the *amban* and then report to the emperor beforehand. For instance, the appointment or removal of a *bka'-blon* or one of the other twelve kinds of important officials, and the confirmation of the reincarnation of a Huthugthu, the Living Buddha in the Tibetan areas, could only be carried out after being approved by the emperor.

The first regent Demo-bde-legs rgyal-mtsho, who reigned after the death of the seventh Dalai Lama, held the office for twenty years; then Tshe-smon-gling khri-chen ngag-dbang-tshul-khrims came into power for fifteen years; then the eighth Dalai Lama 'Jam-dpal rgya-mtsho reigned together with Kun-bde-gling rgyal-tshod huthugthu bstan-pa'i-mgon-po for nineteen years. After the eighth Dalai Lama died, Kun-lde-gling bstan-pa'i-mgon-po carried on his reign for another nine years; then Demo huthugthu 'jings-med-rgyal-mtsho came into power for nine years; then Tshe-smon-gling huthugthu 'jam-dpal tshul-khrims held power for twenty-five years. After he was relieved of his post, Panchen Erdnis Bstan-pa'i nyi-ma assumed the reins of government for nine months; then Rwa'-sgreng huthugthu ngag-dbang ye-she tshul-khrims took the reins for eighteen years (later he was compelled to flee to the hinterland of China, for he was on bad terms with the leaders of the 'Bras-spungs Monastery and a rebellion was being instigated against him). Then Dbang-phyug rgyal-po came into power for three years; after him Demo huthugthu Mkhyen-rab dbang-phyug held power for eight years; then the twelfth Dalai Lama 'Phrin-las rgya-mtsho took the reins for three years. When he died, Rje-drung ngag-dbang dpal-ldan came into power for twelve years; then Demo huthugthu 'phrin-las-rab-rgyas ruled for ten years; and after him the thirteenth Dalai Lama assumed the reins of government.

9. The Encroachment of Imperialists upon Tibet, and How Reactionary Elements of the Upper Strata in Tibet Betrayed Their Country

While strengthening the rule of the Tibetan local regime headed by the Dalai Lama, the Qing Emperor Qian Long drove all the Gurkha invaders out of Tibet and took a series of measures that served to defend our border regions and contributed much to the national unification. But from the year when the Qing Emperor Jia Qing came to the throne, the Fire Dragon year of the thirteenth cycle of the Tibetan calendar (A.D. 1796), he intensified the exploitation and oppression of the people at home, but could not effectively fight back in self-defence against foreign aggressors. Besides, the economy and the political and military forces of our country were declining. All these provided opportunities for the British imperialists to invade our hinterland and conduct reconnaissance and aggressive activities in our border regions, and also for the imperialists to encroach on Tibet. The Opium War, launched in the Iron Rat year of the fourteenth cycle, the twentieth year of the reign of Emperor Dao Guang in the Qing Dynasty (A.D. 1840), reduced China to a state of semicolonialism and semifeudalism. The imperialist powers invaded and occupied Chinese territory, and the Chinese landlord class headed by the emperor, as well as the bureaucrat-bourgeoisie, exploited the people more cruelly. The Chinese people fell into an abyss of misery. This led to a series of peasant uprisings across the country, which dealt heavy blows to the crumbling Qing court's regime. At the same time, broad masses of Tibetan slaves and serfs stood up in revolt, and many of them escaped from their homeland. The number of wandering people in Tibet was increasing. The once prosperous villages were desolated and uninhabited. Under the circumstances, the Tibetan polity based on the merging of religious and secular rule, like an exhausted oil-lamp, began to decline.

In the Wood Sheep year of the fifteenth cycle (A.D. 1895), the thirteenth Dalai Lama took over the reins of the local government upon coming of age. In the Water Hare year of the fifteenth cycle (A.D. 1903), the forces of the British imperialists invaded the border region of Gam-'bras (in the area of Yadong). The next year, Britain and tsarist Russia held secret negotiations, by which Britain acknowledged Afghanistan as being in the Russian sphere of influence and Russia in turn acknowledged Tibet being in the British sphere. In the same year, the British forces stepped up the invasion of Tibet, but were repelled by the broad masses of Tibetan people and some of the upper-ranking patriots. The central government of the Qing court, however, was so weak and incompetent in the face of imperialist invasion that it let the Tibetan local administration sign an unequal treaty with Britain. The thirteenth Dalai Lama, taken in by Russia's schemes and intrigues, dreamed of separating Tibet from China with the help of tsarist Russia and founding an "Independent State of Tibet" under the protection of the tsar. But it soon happened that Russia was defeated by Japan in a war for supremacy over East Asia. Russia became weak politically and militarily, and it was for a time not in a position to covet other countries' territories. Thus, the thirteenth Dalai Lama's dream did not come true. Then Zhao Erfeng, the *amban* and commissioner of Sichuan and Yunnan borderland affairs, and other corrupt officials of the Qing court staged an armed suppression of the uprisings at Sde-dge, Batang, and Litang in Sichuan and other places. Not long after this the Qing court abolishd the title of the thirteenth Dalai Lama and tried to appoint another person to replace him. All these measures taken by the Qing court did much harm to Han-Tibetan solidarity, and British imperialists, taking advantage of this, deceived the thirteenth Dalai Lama by promising to recognize his title of Dalai and help him to found an independent Tibet. Thus the Dalai once again dreamed of separating Tibet from our motherland and founding an "Independent State of Tibet" with the help of British imperialism, the enemy deeply hated by the Tibetan people. This time he was again deceived by imperalism.

In order to invade and occupy the territories of other nations, imperialists throughout history have tempted upper-ranking people and intellectual circles in those nations with idealistic terms such as "national pride" in an attempt to draw them over to their side. Finally, with so-called "economic and military aid," they apply the noose. Even today, there are some people who have not taken lessons from the thirteenth Dalai Lama's experience and who still dream of an "Independent State of Tibet." We really don't know when they will wake up. Surely the invasion and three-year rule over Tibet by Tshe-dbang rab-brtan, the chieftain of the Dzungar Mongols, should be proof enough that deception under the banners of "religion" and "nation" can only lead to the loss of political power.

10. The Launching of Armed Rebellion by Reactionary Upper Strata Elements Under the Signboard of Religion and Nation, and the Abrogation of the Polity Based on the Merging of Religious and Secular Rule

In the Earth Ox year of the sixteenth cycle (A.D. 1949), the Chinese People's Liberation Army (PLA), under the leadership of the Chinese Communist Party, liberated all Chinese territory except Tibet and Taiwan. The founding of the Poeple's Republic of China was proclaimed on October 1 in the same year. The Central People's Government decided to dispatch PLA units to liberate the people of various nationalities in Tibet from imperialist influence and the oppression of feudal serfdom. Simultaneously, the Central Government took a series of measures for talks with the Tibetan local government on the peaceful liberation of Tibet. Nevertheless, due to the fact that the British and American imperialists set up all kinds of obstructions, the consultation on the peaceful liberation of Tibet was not carried out. A handful of Tibetan reactionary high-ranking officials even took the fourteenth Dalai Lama under duress to the border town of Yadong, where they were ready to set up a so-called "independent state" with the support of imperialists. This move instantly aroused a determined opposition from the masses of Tibetan people, patriotic people in the mid and upper strata, and some Tibetan monasteries including the three great ones. Thereupon, the former local government of Tibet, under the pressure of the patriotic force, promised to hold talks with the Central People's Government. When the fourteenth Dalai Lama took over the power, he sent a five-member plenipotentiary delegation headed by Nga-phod Ngag-dbang 'jigs-med to Beijing in February 1951 for negotiation on the peaceful liberation of Tibet. It took less than a month for both sides to reach an agreement on many important problems.

The "Agreement of the Central People's Government and the Local Government of Tibet on Measures for the Peaceful Liberation of Tibet" was signed in Beijing on May 23, 1951. Not long after that, the fourteenth Dalai Lama returned to Lhasa from Yadong. On October 26 of that year, the PLA units arrived in Lhasa and met with a warm welcome from Tibetan secular and clerical people. This agreement was a heavy blow to the imperialists who plotted to invade and take Tibet under their control. It served as a new basis for the unity between Tibetan and Han nationalities and between Tibetan and other Chinese nationalities, and strengthened the unity among the Tibetan people themselves; and it spurred Tibet to a great development in the political, economic, cultural and populational fields.

After their coming into Tibet, the PLA soldiers and officers strictly observed discipline and adhered to the government policies toward nationalities and religion. Their good deeds won the Tibetan people's trust and love for the Communist Party of China, Mao Zedong, and the PLA. Many upper strata people came to realize that the Tibetans could achieve a brilliant future only by taking the socialist road through democratic reform alongside other nationalities under the leadership of the Communist Party of China. Under the circumstances, in 1956, a Preparatory Committee for the Autonomous Region of Tibet was established. Meanwhile, not only did the broad masses of the Tibetan people show their desire for democratic reform, but some people in the mid and upper strata also provided their support for the comprehensive transformation of the old Tibetan social system.

Nevertheless, a handful of die-hard Tibetan officals in the mid and upper strata pretended to support the democratic reform, but in private called secret meetings for scheming against it, distributed leaflets, and convened conferences of the puppet People's Congress of Tibet. In a word, they took various measures to prevent the reform in order to maintain the Tibetan polity based on the merging of religious and secular rule. They not only impeded the reform in political, economic, and military fields, but also misguided the populace ideologically. They took every opportunity of religious meeting to whip up antisocialism sentiments. They said that politics and religion were like a bird's two wings, both of which must be used simultaneously when flying; that the New Tibet must be prosperous in both political and religious affairs; that Tibetans were adherents of Buddhism and followers of Bodhisattva Avalokitesvara; that with only a prosperous secular life but without religious belief, the Tibetans would not have a happy next life; that all governments in the world levied taxes, but that only the Tibetan local government and monasteries deemed the taxes they levied as donations collected from the people to support monasteries and monks for the purpose of promoting the taxpayers' well-being in this life and the next; and so on. With these arguments, they were making politico-ideological preparations for rebelling against their motherland in due time.

The rebellion staged by a handful of reactionary elements in the Tibetan upper strata essentially differed from the conflicts that took place within the Tibetan ruling class in the past. It was a decisive battle between the broad masses of the liberated Tibetan labouring people led by the Communist Party of China and the minority reactionary elements in the upper strata. This struggle developed from bloodless political conflict to bloody battle. In the rebellion, the three kinds of Tibetan manorial lords—local government officials, monasterial leaders, and serf owners—formed an alliance with each other. Their alliance was decided by the class nature of the Tibetan politico-religious system, not by accidental conditions. Historical evidence shows us clearly the class nature, the reactionism, and the duplicity of Tibet's politico-religious system at that time.

When the rebellion was suppressed, the mountain weighing on the back of the Tibetan labouring people for centuries was overthrown, the economic basis of the evil politico-religious system was wiped away, and thus the various religious privileges based on the system were dealt heavy blows. The broad masses of the Tibetan people, including some of the monks in monasteries, gained their personal freedom, and the productive forces in Tibet were liberated. The people came to realize that it was due to the politico-religious system that they had led a miserable life for generations. Since then, the people who really believe in religion can take part in religious activities as they like. If they observe the state's law, their happy life is ensured. Ended forever is the centuries-old misery of the Tibetan people. They have become the masters of their own land. With each passing year Tibet has achieved greater and greater progress in productive, economic, and cultural spheres, and the population has increased. This has brought about marked changes for the better in the region. The once poor and backward old Tibet has now begun to advance to a happy and prosperous new Tibet.

III. Conclusion

It can be seen that prior to the formation and development of the Tibetan politico-religious system, secular rule and clerical rule were separated, each with its own leaders. But afterwards the Tibetan polity developed into a merger of secular and clerical rule under identical leadership representing both sides. The emergence of this system was not a result of sudden change, but was a historical phenomenon profoundly based on social conditions and class origin.

(1) The historical conditions in which the politico-religious system emerged had close connection with the existence and diffusion of Buddhism in Tibet. It was in the early seventh century, in the reign of Srong-btsan Sgam-po, that Buddhism was introduced into Tibet. From that time on to the reign of Khri-srong-lde-btsan, when the Buddhist clerical institution began to be set up, in a period of more than a hundred years, the Tibetan people held both Bon and Buddhist belief, but most of them were Bonists. At that time although there were Buddhists in Tibet, there were neither professional monks (or nuns) nor monasteries big enough for monks to reside in. The Buddhists had no privileges, and Buddhism was unable to compete with the Bon religion. When *btsan-po* (king) Khri-srong-lde-btsan came of age, he took power. The *btsan-po* invited from India several panditas and prominent Buddhist scholars, such as Padmasambhava and 'Santaraksita, and built up the Bsam-yas Monastery and other Buddhist monasteries. He also had many Buddhist texts translated from Sanskrit and Han into Tibetan. In an experiment to find out whether the Buddhist clerical

institution could be set up in Tibet, seven intelligent young men were made to take the oath to convert to Buddhism and became monks, and not long afer this the number of monks increased to three hundred.

When 'Santaraksita served as *mkhan-po* (abbot), all the daily necessities of the monks were supplied by the *btsan-po*'s storehouse. Afterwards, considering that the *btsan-po*'s economic help could not be everlasting, especially after his death, and that his storehouse might not be able to support them, Khri-srong-lde-btsan stipulated the amount of monthly and yearly supplies of food, salt, butter, cloth, and paper for panditas, *mkhan-pos*, monks, and those who were practising Buddhist cultivation. Each monk was granted three households of serfs, who were responsible for his daily necessities. After that it was no longer the *btsan-po*, but the government that was responsible for paying the monks' expenses. This reform was a measure taken by the *btsan-po* to secure the monks' living resources and for the government to show its respect to the monks and protect them, for according to Buddhist regulations they were not allowed to engage in productive activities and thus were not able to support themselves. If the reformed institution had been carried forward and the living standard of monks had been kept within limits, high-ranking monks would not have become manorial lords who held political power in their hands, and the system under which both secular and religious powers were held by religious personages of the upper strata would not have been set up.

But this institution, under which the government supplied daily necessities to the monks, could be carried out only if the number of monks rmained small. If the number of monks became too great for the government to support, providing for them would become an economic burden and arouse bad feelings among the officials. Besides, if the government's income could not cover its outlay, the economic burden would weigh heavily on the backs of the people. As a result, the people would become poorer and poorer, and the government, without a solid economic foundation, would certainly fall apart.

In the reigns of *btsan-po* Khri-srong-lde-btsan, Mu-ne btsan-po, and Khri-lde-srong-btsan in succession, the number of monks was rather small, so the above-mentioned institution was kept on. The monks owned some slave households, but did not possess farm, pastureland, or livestock. They were slave owners who got their subsidies from the government. Later, in the reign of *btsan-po* Ral-pa-chan, the Mtshur-phur Monastery at Stod-lung and four minor temples near Lhasa were entitled to possess farms, pastureland, livestock, and slaves. This measure lightened the government's load and ensured the monks' resources, no matter what changes the government might undergo. Due to the reform, some Buddhist monks were transformed from slave owners without farms, pastureland, or livestock into serf owners possessing farms, pastureland, livestock, and serfs. The new institution developed and became consolidated. In a period of more than four hundred years, the monasteries and high-ranking monks of various religious sects in Tibet came to own a great number of farms, pastureland, livestock, and serfs. This was the historical condition and economic foundation on which the Tibetan politico-religious system was based.

(2) The social base and the class origin of the Tibetan politico-religious system are as follows. On the one hand, the few upper-ranking monks in various religious sects were transformed from slave owners into serf owners, and the majority of monks became poorer and poorer under their oppression and exploitation; on the other hand, all Buddhist monks lived on the donations of Buddhist adherents. Under the feudal serf system, the broad masses of serfs had to endure unbearable miseries caused by the exploitation and oppression of the serf owners. In order to escape their miserable life, some of the serfs left their homes and became monks, hoping to eke out a living by relying

on others' donations. Thus Buddhist monks were divided into two classes, upper and lower. The upper-ranking monks were very strong economically; they held a part of the Tibetan economic lifeline in their hands through renting their farmland to farmers, collecting land rents, practising usury, and doing business. Some of them made use of influential local political cliques to back their economic status; some held political power directly in their hands. In these two ways, they protected their religious power and economic privileges. This was the class origin out of which the Tibetan politico-religious system grew.

(3) When the Tibetan polity based on the merging of religious and secular rule reached its highest stage, the upper-ranking religious personages began to hold political power. It began with the Sa-skya sect; then came in succession the Phag-gru Bka'-brgyud sect, the Karma Bka'-brgyud sect, and the Dge-lugs sect. In that historical period, the various religious sects were in rivalry. Their main conflicts were the struggle for manorial estates and serfs, while the conflicts caused by their different points of religious view were but secondary. In the struggle for monasterial manors and serfs, the ruling classes of various sects always took advantage of the religious beliefs of the people, which was characterzied by locality and ethnicity, for their own purposes. And when the rivalries among the rulers of various sects became critical, foreign aggressive powers always made use of them to magnify the national split and in this way were able to penetrate into Tibet. Whenever a religious sect got the upper hand and gained control over a large part of Tibet, it oppressed others with the political and economic power in their hands. This was caused, in the final analysis, by the faulty economic policies of previous Tibetan local governments with regard to the monks: the government had not sufficient economic strength to support the monks and thus granted them the economic privileges of possessing and managing farms, pastureland, livestock, and serfs.

Now, in socialist China, the broad masses of the Tibetan people have been liberated from the feudal politico-religious system, and they are enjoying personal freedom and leading a happy life. The monks who really adhered to Buddhism were also liberated under the principle that clerical rule had to be separated from secular rule. If they are patriotic and law-abiding, they will enjoy freedom of religious belief and the concern shown by the government for their living. The mistakes caused by the Left-leaning line in the past policy towards religious belief were discovered and corrected in time by the Central Government.

I lived under the Tibetan politico-religious system for many years and was entitled "Living Buddha." With the help of the Chinese Communist Party, I have participated in revolutionary work and studied the theory of Maxism-Leninism as well as social and natural scientific works and ancient Tibetan annals. Now I have a better understanding of dialectical materialism and historical materialism and thus have gained a wider field of vision. I have come to realize that when I was a monk in the monastery, I was completely ignorant of social evolution and social development. Compared with my life at that time, my progress today is satisfactory. I realize that one's level of understanding can be raised by studying and analyzing histori-cal events, annals, and relics and by learning lessons from the past. This book attempts to present my point of view on the history of the Tibetan polity based on the merging of religious and secular rule. Readers are welcome to give their comments and opinions on it.

IV. Bibliography

References in the Tibetan Language

1. *Sba-bzhed* (*Records of the Bsam-yas Monastery*), three different editions.

2. Tshal-si-tu dge-ba'i-blo-gros (also called Kun-dga' rdo-rje), *Deb-ther dmar-po* (*Red Annals*).

3. Pan-chen Bsod-nams Grags-pa, *Deb-dmar-gsar-ma, Rgyal-rabs lde-mig* (*A Divine Key to the Royal Lineage,* or *New Red Annals*).

4. 'Gos-lo-tsa-ba gzhon-nu-dpal, *Deb-ther Sngon-po* (*Blue Annals*).

5. Dpa'-bo gtsug-lag phreng-ba, *Mkhas-pa'i Dga'-ston* (*A Feast for Wise Men*).

6. Stag-tshang-pa dpal-'byor bzang-po, *Rgya-bod-yig-tshang* (*Analects on the Historical Relations Between the Hans and Tibetans*).

7. The Fifth Dalai Lama, *Dpyid-kyi-rgyal-mo'i glu-dbyangs* (*Records of Tibetan Kings and Ministers*).

8. Thu'u-kwan blo-bzang chos-kyi nyi-ma, *Grub-mtha' shel-gyi me-long* (*Origins and Development of Various Religious sects*).

9. Sum-pa mkhan-po ye-shes dpal-'byor, *Dpa'-bsam ljon-bzang* (*History of the Treasure Tree of Buddhism*).

10. Dpal-mang dkon-mchog-rgyal-mtshan, *Rgya-bod-hor-sog-gi-lo-rgyus* (*Concise History of the Han, Tibetan, Hor, and Mongol People*).

11. Mgon-po-skyabs, Rgya-nag chos-byung (*History of Buddhism in the Han Areas*).

12. Jo-nang taranatha, *Gya-gar chos-byung* (*History of Buddhism in India*).

13. Ri-bo-che dpon-tshang tshe-dbang-rgyal, *Lho-rong chos-byung* (*Religious History of Lho-rong*).

14. Gu-ge mkhan-chen ngag-dbang grags-pa, *Mnga'-ris chos-byung* (*Religious History of Mnga'-ris*).

15. Sog-po dam-chos rgya-mtsho, *Hor-chos-byung* (*Religious History of Mongolia*).

16. Kun-dga'-bsod-nams, *Sa-skya dgung-rabs* (*Sa-skya's Lineal Description*).

17. 'Be-lo-tsa-ba tshe-dbang kun-khyab, *Karma-kam-tshang-chos-byung* (*History of the Karma Sect*).

18. Brag-sgom-pa bstan-pa rab-rgyas, *Mdo-smad-chos-byung, deb-ther rgya-mtsho* (*Political and Religious History of Amdo*).

19. Sde-srid Sangs-rgyas rgya-mtsho, *Bedura-ser-po* (*The Yellow Glaze—Religious History of the Yellow Sect*).

20. Sde-srid Sangs-rgyas rgya-mtsho, *Khrims-yig dwangs-shel me-long* (*Collected Works of Buddhist Laws*).

21. 'Jog-po ngag-dbang bstan-'dzin, *Tshal gung-thang dkar-chag* (*Catalogue of Tshal gung-thang*).

22. Mkhas-pa dkar-shag-pa, *Sde-pa rin-spungs-pa'i gdong-rabs* (*Rin-spungs-pa's Lineal Description*).

23. The First Dalai Lama Dge-'dun grub, *'Dul-ba lung-sde bzhi'i gleng-gzhi phyogs-bsdus* (*Symposium on the Four Sets of Buddhist Precepts*).

24. Byang-chub rgyal-mtshan, *Bka'-chems deb-ther* (*Collection of Deceased King's Teachings*).

25. Rwa yes-shes seng-ge, *Rwa-lo-tsa-ba'i rnam-thar* (*Biography*

of Rdo-rje-grags, the Sutra Translator of the Twa Group).

26. *Mkha'-'gro yes-shes mtsho-rgyal rnam-thar* (*Biography of Mkha'-'gro yes-shes mtsho-rgyal*).

27. Cha-har dge-bshes blo-bzang tshul-khrims, *Tsong-kha-pa'i rnam-thar* (*Biography of Tsong-kha-pa*).

28. Ser-smad mkhan-po grags-pa mkhas-grub, *Dge-ldan khri-thog rim-byon gyi rnam-thar* (*Biographies of Successive Hierarchs of the Yellow Sect*).

29. G·yang-ba-chos-rje dkon-mchog-skyabs, *Ta'-la'i bla-ma Sku-phreng dang-po dge-'dun-grub-kyi rnam-thar* (*Biography of the First Dalai Lama Dge-'dun grub*).

30. Pan-chen bsod-nams grags-pa, *Dge-'dun rgya-mtsho'i rnam-thar* (*Biography of the Second Dalai Lama Dge-'dun rgya-mtsho*).

31. The Fifth Dalai Lama, *Bsod-nams rgya-mtsho'i rnam-thar* (*Biography of the Third Dalai Lama Bsod-nams rgya-mtsho*)

32. The Fifth Dalai Lama, *Yon-tan rgya-mtsho'i rnam-thar* (*Biography of the Fourth Dalai Lama Yon-tan rgya-mtsho*).

33. The Fifth Dalai Lama, Ta'la'i bla-ma lnga-pa'i rang-rnam (*Autobiography—Rosy Clouds*).

34. Sde-srid sangs-rgyas rgya-mtsho, *Ta'la'i bla-ma lnga-pa'i rnam-thar* (*Biography of the Fifth Dalai Lama*).

35. Sde-srid sangs-rgyas rgya-mtsho, *Ta'la'i bla-ma lnga-pa'i gser-gdung 'dzam-gling rgyan-gcig-gi dkar-chag* (*Stupa and Relics of the Fifth Dalai Lama*).

36. Sde-srid sangs-rgyas rgya-mtsho, *Ta'la'i bla-ma drug-pa'i rnam-thar* (*Biography of the Sixth Dalai Lama*), and *Ta'la'i bla-ma drug-pa's gsang-ba'i rnam-thar* (*The Legendary of the Sixth Dalai Lama*).

37. Lcang-skya rol-pa'i rdo-rje, *Ta'la'i bla-ma bdun-pa'i rnam-thar* (*Biography of the Seventh Dalai Lama*).

38. Demo huthugthu bde-legs rgya-mtsho, *Ta'la'i bla-ma brgyad-pa'i rnam-thar* (*Biography of the Eighth Dalai Lama 'Jam-dpal rgya-mtsho*).

39. Phur-lcog yongs-'dzin byams-pa tshul khrims, *Ta'la'i bla-ma bcu-gsum-pa'i rnam-thar* (*Biography of the Thirteenth Dalai Lama Thub-bstan rgya-mtsho*).

40. The Fifth Panchen Erdenis blo-bzang ye-shes, *Panchen Bzhi-pa' blo-bzang chos-kyi rgyal-mtshan gyi rnam-thar* (*Biography of the Fourth Panchen Erdenis Blo-bzang chos-kyi rgyal-mtshan*).

41. *Pan-chen lnga-pa blo-bzang ye-shes kyi rang rnam* (*Autobiography of the Fifth Panchen Erdenis Blo-bzang ye-shes*).

42. The Second 'Jam-dbyangs bzhad-pa 'jigs-med dbang-po, *'Jam-dbyangs bzhad-pa dang-po ngag-dbang-brtson-'grus kyi rnam-thar* (*Biography of the First 'Jam-dbyangs bzhad-pa ngag-dbang brtson-'grus*).

43. Thu'u-kwan chos-kyi nyi-ma, *Lcang-skya huthugthu rol-pa'i rdo-rje rnam-thar* (*Biography of Lcang-skya huthugthu rol-pa'i rdo-rje*).

44. *Historical Documents About Ancient Tibet from Dunhuang.*

45. The Rubbing from the Memorial Stele to Ngan-lam stag-sgra klu-gong in Front of the Potala Palace at Lhasa.

46. The Rubbing from the Stele in the Dkar-chung Monastery.

47. The Rubbing from the Stone Stele in the Mtshur-phu' Monastery at Stod-lung.

48. Mdo-mkhar zhabs-drung tshe-ring dbang-rgyal, *Mi-dbang-rtogs-brjod* (*Biography of Pho-lha-nas*).

49. Rdo-ring bstan-'dzin dpal-'byor, *Rdo-ring pandita'i mi-rabs-kyi-byung-ba brjod-pa* (*Genealogy of Rdo-ring Pandita*).

APPENDIX A

The Thirteen-Article Ordinance for the More Efficient Governing of Tibet

(Drawn up by Tshe-ring and others; adopted by the joint conference of the *amban*, the local government of Tibet, and the representatives of the Three Grand Monasteries; and approved by the Emperor Qian Long.)

Tshe-ring, imperial envoy, grand tutor to the crown prince, minister of the Department of War, censor of the Court of Censors, provincial military governor of Sichuan in charge of provisions and funds for troops;

Zhao Hui, vice-minister of the Ministry of the Interior;

Shu Lai, *amban* (imperial representative in Tibet), imperial bodyguard, commander of the palace guards, vice-minister of the Ministry in charge of public works;

Namu Zhale, minister of the Ministry of the Interior;

Ban-de, vice military governor in charge of Tibetan affairs;

Bahada, vice minister of the judiciary;

Jie Bu, director of the Department of National Minorities Affairs;

Fu-lang-ah, secretary; and

Duke Pandita, a *bka'-blon* appointed by His Imperial Majesty, were ordered to work out a complete ordinance by the Great Emperor. According to investigations, 'Gyur-med rnams-rgyal was an evil-minded man. He did not hold respect for the Dalai Lama, but nursed a hatred against him. He killed his own brother, put his own sister under house arrest, and behaved brutally and cruelly to others. He disregarded law and discipline and launched revolts. All his illegal acts were witnessed by the two *amban* and were hated by all the Tibetan people. In oder to ensure the Dalai Lama's safety, the two *amban* had no other alternative but to adopt the last measure. After submitting a report to the Great Emperor, they summoned 'Gyur-med rnams-rgyal to Khrom-gzigs-sgang (the *amban's* government office) and had him put to death. The Great Emperor understood from the memorial to the throne by the Dalai Lama and the two *amban* that the lawless person had already been executed and, in order to deal with problems arising from the incident more smoothly, ordered that the imperial envoy and other high-ranking officials go to Tibet and have a thorough consultation with the Dalai Lama, Duke Pandita, and other high-ranking officials, so that the old system might be kept on. The important thing is to maintain the Tibetan region a stable social order, let all the people follow the Dalai Lama more conscientiously, and let each be properly provided for and share peace and happiness. All the Tibetan monks and lay people should be grateful to the Emperor's special kindness and, from now on, should obey all the orders issued by the Emperor for the benefit of the Tibetan people.

We gathered together and, after consulting with each other thoroughly and referring to the old system, worked out an ordinance as follows:

1. According to the old system, a new *bka'-blon* should be appointed. In the past, there were four *bka'-blon.* But Bka'-blon 'Brong-rtse-ba was already dismissed by 'Gyur-med rnams-rgyal due to his losing the sight of both eyes, so there remaind only three *bka'-blon*—Pandita, Tshe-ring dbang-rgyal, and Srid-gcod tshe-bstan. Pandita has already received a special imperial decree to the effect that he remain in the post of *bka'-blon*, so it is not necessary to discuss his problem. Both Tshe-ring dbang-rgyal and Srid-gcod tshe-bstan were transferred to other places by 'Gyur-med rnams-rgyal before Blo-bzang bkra-shis and his traitorous clique staged the rebellion, and they were not at

Lhasa when the rebellion occurred. Neither of them committed any mistakes at their post, nor had anything to do with the rebels; in addition, they were *bka'-blon* originally assigned by the Emperor, so it is appropriate for them to remain at the *bka'-blon* posts. As to the post left vacant by 'Brong-rtse-ba, a prestigious and capable Yellow Sect lama should be promoted to assume the office. This will be of great benefit to the monks and lay people. Among the present three *bka'-blon*, Pandita is a duke, the other two have been granted by the Emperor the title of *dza-sag*, the title of the first degree among the *the-ci* (governors). It would not conform to the system if the newly appointed monk *bka'-blon* is not granted an honorific title. Therefore, the Emperor would be requested to grant a title of *dza-sag* to the Grand Lama newly appointed monk *bka'-blon*, so that he may have an equal standing with other *bka'-blon*.

2. The *bka'-blon* should handle their official business in their government offices. The *bka'-blon* used to handle public business in their government offices. But since Pho-lha-nas controlled political power, all the *bka'-blon* have handled public business at their residences instead. Furthermore, they did not trust the *mgron-gnyer* (official in charge of public relations), *bi-qig-qi* (secretaries), and other officials who were authorized by the government, but arbitrarily assigned their trusted followers to the posts of *mgron-gnyer* and *bi-qig-qi*. This was how *mgron-gnyer* Blo-bzang bkra-shis could usurp authority and muster a band of rebels. Now that all the *bka'-blon* have been reappointed, they should go to the government offices to do their business in compliance with the old regulations. All the officials appointed illegally by individual *bka'-blon* should be dismissed, and public business should be handled by the *mgron-gnyer* and other officials appointed by the government. The *bka'-blon* should not let personal considerations interfere with their execution of public duties. It is their duty to handle minor local affairs properly after consulting among themselves. On all

important or emergent problems, the *bka'-blon* should ask the Dalai Lama and *amban* for instructions and act as they are ordered. The *bka'-blon* should act in accordance with regulations whenever they ask to use the Dalai Lama's or *amban*'s official seals. Henceforth if any *bka'-blon* does not behave in compliance with this ordinance but does things in his own way, other *bka'-blon* must report his illegal activities to the Dalai Lama and *amban*, so that they can report to the Emperor and have the lawbreaker punished.

3. *Bka'-blon* have no right to appoint *sde-pa* (local officials) without authorization, such as a *rdzong-dpon* or the chief director of a manor. It is the duty of a *sde-pa* in every part of Tibet to administer his district and take good care of the people there. Since 'Gyur-med rnams-rgyal took over power, he appointed arbitrarily his trusted subordinates as *sde-pa*. They do not hold the posts themselves, but dispatch their house slaves to act for them instead. Such a practice has done much harm to the local people. From now on, whenever a *sde-pa* or a local official is to be appointed, the *bka'-blon* should discuss the matter and report to the Dalai Lama and the *amban* beforehand. The *bka'-blon* can assign a *sde-pa* or a local official to the post only after receiving the Dalai Lama's and the *amban*'s official documents affixed with their seals. All the present *sde-pas* who are house slaves acting for their masters should be dismissed, and new ones will be appointed. After 'Gyur-med rnams-rgyal was killed, Duke Pandita sent *sde-pa* to replace those who had been involved in the rebellion. But those appointments were carried out in a hurry and hence their tenure of office was temporary. If any one of them is found incompetent as a *sde-pa*, the *bka'-blon* should report him to the Dalai Lama and the *amban*, so that a new one may be appointed.

4. Detailed regulations concerning the dismissal and punishment of officials should be worked out. According to the old system, *sde-pa* were selected from those who had a sound

character and were capable of managing public affairs; and if any one of them was found incompetent for his work or violating the law wantonly, he was to be punished. But 'Gyur-med rnams-rgyal acted presumptuously; he dismissed without authorization all those whom he disliked, confiscated their properties arbitrarily, and confused truth and falsehood; consequently complaints were heard everywhere. From now on, when a *sde-pa* is to be whipped for a small crime or his eyes are to be gouged out or one of his limbs cut off for theft or other serious crimes, *bka'-blon* should decide the case justly according to law. When a lama or a nobleman has committed a crime, his property should be confiscated; as to the ones who have committed capital crimes, the *bka'-blon* and *mda'-dpon* should investigate their cases impartially, draw up their punishment respectively, ask the Dalai Lama and the *amban* for instructions, and act in compliance with their instructions.

5. The assignment of high-ranking lamas and *mkhan-po* should be carried out according to the old regulations. In past, the *mkhan-po* and high-ranking lamas of a monastery were assigned by the Dalai Lama in the light of the size of the monastery and of the lamas' merits and ability. But after 'Gyur-med rnams-rgyal controlled political power, he gave himself a free hand to appoint or remove *mkhan-po* or high-ranking lamas without consulting the Dalai Lama. Such practices were unlawful. From now on only the Dalai Lama has the right to appoint or dismiss a *mkhan-po* of a monastery. No *bka'-blon* may act contrary to this regulation. If any lama breaks the law, the *bka'-blon* should report the case to the Dalai Lama and act according to his instructions.

6. Supernumerary personnel should be dismissed. According to the old regulations, officials such as the *mgron-gnyer, phyag-mdzod, gzim-dpon*, and *gsol-dpon*, were appointed only to serve the Dalai Lama. Later, when Pho-lha-nas was granted the title of "King," he followed suit and appointed his relatives and

friends to various important posts. Now the *bka'-blon* are not kings, and it is improper for them to install important officials. All those installed illegally should be dismissed. Only two *mgron-gnyer* and one *bi-qig-qi* are to be installed in Bka'-shag.

7. One more *mda'-dpon* is to be installed. According to the old regulations, *bka'-blon* are in charge of local civil affairs, while *mda'-dpon* are responsible for military affairs. Each has his own duty. This regulation should be maintained. But the Gtsang region is quite small and has three *mda'-dpon*, while the Dbus region is quite large but has only one *mda'-dpon;* when he is away on an errand or falls ill, there is no commander to take charge of military affairs. For instance, when *mda'-dpon* Dar-rgyas bkra-shis was dispatched on an errand by 'Gyur-med rnams-rgyal to Hala-usu (Nagchu region), there was nobody in the Dbus region in command of troops, so that the rebel leader Blo-bzang bkra-shis could gather his troops to create confusion in the region. From now on, one more *mda'-dpon* should be installed in the Dbus region, so that if one *mda'-dpon* is dispatched on an errand, there will be still one remaining to take charge of regional security and to protect the Dalai Lama. From now on, when moving troops to safeguard outposts of the tax office, *mda'-dpon* should act according to the official documents issued by the Dalai Lama and the *amban*. *Mda'-dpon* also ought to pay attention to the local situation; when it becomes serious, they should report to the imperial envoys (*amban*) and act according to their instructions. As to Lcang-lo-can-pa, the former *mda'-dpon* of the Gtsang region, investigation reveals that 'Gyur-med rnams-rgyal intended to do him harm and so dismissed him from his service without authorization. Therefore, Lcang-lo-can-pa should be rehabilitated and reappointed the *mda'-dpon* of the Gtsang region.

8. Each *bka'-blon* and *mda'-dpon* is to be given an imperial diploma. All the *bka'-blon* and *mda'-dpon* are high-ranking officials in charge of the Dalai Lama's security and local civil

or military affairs. Each of them holds a responsible position, so the Dalai Lama and *amban* should request that the Emperor grant each of them an imperial diploma as an honour. The name list of all the present *bka'-blon* and *mda'-dpon* is to be sent to the Central Government, so that diplomas will be granted to them. In the future, whenever a *bka'-blon*'s or *mda'-dpon*'s position is vacant, the *amban*, after having consulted with the Dalai Lama and jointly selected a qualified candidate, should request the Emperor's approval and a diploma for him. Henceforth, the *bka'-blon* or *mda'-dpon* who has not the greatest esteem for the Dalai Lama or has committed a crime and is not qualified to manage local affairs should be dismissed after the Dalai Lama has jointly with the *amban* sent a memorial to the throne to impeach him, and the diploma granted him should be taken back.

9. The people should not be held as private property. According to the old system, all the people belonged to the Dalai Lama, and the Dalai Lama allocated a certain amount of taxation and corvée on the people in accordance with the size of the area and the number of households for the expenses of the Buddhist ceremonies of the Yellow Sect and for the maintenance of monks' lives. But since Pho-lha-nas and his son 'Gyur-med rnams-rgyal controlled political power, they not only forcibly occupied many areas they liked, but also bestowed wantonly on those who were in their favour, and gave them documents to exempt them from taxation and corvée, while levied heavy taxes or allocated various forms of corvée on those out of their favour. The *bka'-blon* and *mda'-dpon* should jointly check the files to find out which households were given by 'Gyur-med rnams-rgyal to his followers without proper reasons and report to the Dalai Lama so that those households may revert to the local government, and all those documents given to his followers to exempt them from taxation should be taken back, and they should pay taxes and do corvée as they did

before. Only the bestowals given to those who really merited rewards are not to be withdrawn. All the newly allotted corvées should be reported to the Dalai Lama and be exempted, so that the people may not be too heavily burdened. Henceforth, when a person has rendered great service and merits a reward, *bka'-blon* and *mda'-dpon* should impartially report to the Dalai Lama and the *amban* and reward the person according to their instructions.

10. *Ula* (unpaid labour) certificates can be issued only by the Dalai Lama. According to the old regulation, only the Dalai Lama could enjoy the corvée supplied by the local people without pay. But after Pho-lha-nas and his son 'Gyur-med rnams-rgyal controlled political power, the old regulation slackened. *Bka'-blon* and *mda'-dpon* have been issuing *ula* certificates without authorization when they send people to Xining, Dajianlu, 'Bar-khams, Mnga'-ris, or other regions to do commercial business. All their food, lodging, and corvée are provided by the localities without pay; consequently, exorbitant taxes and levies of every sort have become too heavy a burden upon the people, and many of them have fled from their home places, wandering up and down the country. Such outmoded regulations and irrational practices must be abolished. Henceforth *bka'-blon* and *mda'-dpon* must not issue *ula* certificates of their own when they send people elsewhere to do commercial business. Whenever *ula* service is needed for official duties, they should report to the Dalai Lama to ask for an official certificate. The *bka'-blon* can issue certificates only when corvées are to be exacted in the neighbourhood.

11. The *bka'-blon* are forbidden to take out and use materials and articles stored in the Dalai Lama's storehouse. According to old regulations, the Dalai Lama's steward manages all the articles in the storehouse. When certain articles are needed for public affairs, *bka'-blon* should report to the Dalai Lama before the articles are taken out. Without the Dalai Lama's written

permission, nobody can take anything out of his storehouse. But since Pho-lha-nas and then 'Gyur-med rnams-rgyal controlled political power, they took all they wanted from the storehouse wantonly without reporting to the Dalai Lama, and what is more, the Dalai Lama was not in a position to draw even a *hada* (ceremonial scarf) from his storehouse for his own use. Such a situation was quite abnormal and ridiculous. Henceforth all will be managed in accordance with old regulations. Without the Dalai Lama's order, nobody can open or close the gate of the storehouse. The Dalai Lama's steward has the right to take articles out of the storehouse for the Dalai Lama's daily use. When the *bka'-blon* want to use the articles in the storehouse for public duties, they should consult among themselves beforehand and then ask the Dalai Lama for instructions. They are strictly forbidden to draw on stock without the Dalai Lama's permission.

12. The Mnga'-ris and Nagchu regions are very important places. Nagchu borders on Qinghai, while Mnga'-ris is contiguous to Dzungar. The chiefs sent to take charge of these regions must be selected and appointed by the Dalai Lama from those who are reliable and prestigious. The Dalai Lama should submit the names of the persons appointed to the Central Government and beg the Emperor to bestow diplomas on them in order to strengthen the borderland security.

13. The Mongols in the 'Dam region should be helped to settle down in accordance with the imperial decree. These Mongols were settled in that region as watchmen by Pho-lha-nas in accordance with an imperial decree. After 'Gyur-med rnams-rgyal was killed, most them ran away from 'Dam to other places in Tibet, for there was nobody taking care of them. These Mongols were not guilty. They led a nomadic life and their customs were quite different from those of Tibetans. An investigation conducted recently among them in accordance with an imperial decree revealed that they would like to return to 'Dam.

So it is our duty to help them to settle down properly. In the past, the 'Dam Mongols were divided into eight banners. The chieftain of each banner was granted a title by 'Gyur-med rnams-rgyal; some were called *zai-sang* and some were *the-ci*. These titles did not conform to the rules. Now it is decided that the present eight chieftains will be given the title of *gu-shan-da*, their eight assistants will be given the title of *zuo-ling-zhang-jing*, and still eight other subordinates will be appointed cavalry captains. They all will be given official caps and uniforms in accordance with rules, and they are under the command of the *amban*. Each chieftain should dispatch ten men (altogether eighty) to Tibet in order to strengthen public security and to protect the Dalai Lama. Their grain rations and wages are to be drawn from the Dalai Lama's storehouse. Their transfers can be carried out only by the *amban*'s documents with official seal. *Bka'-blon* and *mda'-dpon* have no right to order them about. Their dismissal and appointment can be decided by the *amban* only after consultation with Dalai Lama. These Mongols will be checked annually, and those who are diligent, respectful, and submissive will be rewarded, while those who do not abide by the law and discipline will be punished severely.

All the above-mentioned articles were worked out in compliance with the imperial decree for the everlasting peace and happiness of all the monks and lay people in Tibet. They were worked out by the *amban* jointly with the Dalai Lama with reference to the old regulations, and met with approval of the people and the support of Duke Pandita.

All the *bka'-blon*, *mda'-dpon*, *ding-dpon*, and chieftains and all the monks and lay people should obey imperial decrees and offer their absolute devotion to the Dalai Lama. Now the Tibetans shall live and work in peace and contentment, and their descendants surely will enjoy their allotted share of happiness. Under the protection of the Dalai Lama they will enjoy imperial bounty forever.

Anyone who commits a misdemeanour against this Ordinance will be demoted, and anyone who commits a high misdemeanour will be dismissed from office. Let all the people in the Tibetan regions be acquainted with this long-term legal system, abide by it, and never run counter to it.

The following is a list of the participants in the conference.

'Bras-spungs Monastery:

Sangs-rgyas-rdo-rje, a lama from Sgo-mang grva-tshang;

'Jam-dbyangs-phun-tshogs, a lama from Blo-gsal-gling grva-tshang;

Skal-bzang-bde-chen, a lama from Bde-dbyangs grva-tshang;

Sngags-pa-bla-ma ngag-dbang-legs-pa;

'Du-ba bla-ma ngang-dbang-bkra-shis;

Shar-sgo-bla-ma blo-bzang 'jam-dbyangs;

Byes-pa-bla-ma don-grub-rgya-mtsho.

Se-ra Monastery:

Blo-bzang-rgyal-mtshan, a lama from Smad grva-tshang;

Blo-bzang-mkhas-chos, a lama from Byes grva-tshang;

Blo-bzang-chos-'byor, a lama from Sngags-pa grva-tshang;

Dpal-'byor-rgya-mtsho, a lama from Stod-pa grva-tshang.

Dga'-ldan Monastery:

Byang-rtse bla-ma blo-bzang-'phrin-las

Myang-rong-bla-ma byams-pa-rin'dzin.

Dalai Lama's personal attendant Khral-pa dwags-yi, steward Yon-tan-legs-grub, and sutra translator Ngag-dbang-don-grub.

Leading lamas of the Spyi-gsos (the institute in charge of monasterial public property) of the 'Bras-spung Monastery: Blo-bzang-nor-bu and Bsam-grub-rgya-mtsho.

Leading lamas of the Spyi-gsos of the Se-ra Monastery: Blo-bzang-dpal-ldan and Blo-bzang-'phrin-las.

The chief steward of the Dga'-ldan Monastery, Bstan-pa-dar-rgyas.

Bka'-blon Duke Pandita (rdo-ring), *bka'-blon* Tshe-ring-dbang-rgyal (Ra-ka-shar), *bka'-blon* Srid-gcod-tshe-bstan (thun-pa), and *Bka'-blon* Nyi-ma-rgyal-mtshan.

Duke Kun-dga'-bstan-'dzin, Duke 'Gyur-med-dbang-rgyal, and Dza-sag-tai-ji dbang-'dus.

The *mda'-dpon* of the Dbus region: Dar-rgyas-bkra-shis and Bsod-nams-rdo-rje.

The *mda'-dpon* of the Gtsang region: Lcang-lo-can-pa-a-srid, Dpal-tshe tshe-ring-rnam-rgyal, and Ram-pa-ba rab-gtan.

Rtsis-dpon (chief of the auditorial bureau) Mkhas-grub phun-tshogs.

Lha-sa *bla-brang* phyag-mdzod Tshe-dbang-bkra-shis, Dar-mo bkra-shis-rgyal-po, *gsher-dpang* spo-ra-ba ngag-dbang.

Lha-sa *gnyer-tshang* (chief in charge of the Lhasa store-house) Tshe-ring-bkra-shis, security officer Dpal-ldan-tshe-ring, *zhol-gnyer* Mkhar-thodg-bag-gro, Lha-lung-rtse Tshe-ring-rdo-rje, *mi-dpon* Rags-rtsibs tshe-dbang-don-grub, Rtse-mgron rdo-rje-phun-tshogs, *chibs-dpon* Gter-sna tshe-dpal, Mer-mo dbang-'dus-rdo-rje.

Bak'-drung (Bka'-shag secretaries) Tsha-tshul dngos-grub dpal-'bar, Lcags-sprags tshe-dpal, and Zur-khang lha-dbang-dar-rgyas; *rtsa-len* (cashiers) Grong-stod khang-gsar don-grub, Spo-ra-bu tshe-bstan-rnam-rgyal; *rtswa-gnyer* (officers in charge of fodder) Shar-sgo tshe-dbang-rnam-rgyal, Bde-chen bsod-nams-dbang-rgyal; *shing-gnyer* (officer in charge of firewood) Bying-ma lha-bzang-rab-gtan.

March 3, the sixteenth year of the reign of Emperor Qian Long (1751)

APPENDIX B

The Twenty-Nine-Article Ordinance
for the More Efficient Governing of Tibet

1. Considering the drawbacks of the Tibetan institution according to which the incarnations of Living Buddhas and Huthugthus of the Yellow Sect were decided through consulting the oracles of the four Grand Law protectors, the Great Emperor bestowed a golden vase for the purpose of choosing incarnations and stipulated that the "soul boys" of Living Buddhas and Huthugthus shall be chosen by drawing lots from the golden vase. The procedure is as follows. When the soul boys are discovered, their names and dates of birth will be carved in Manchu, Han, and Tibetan scripts on a tablet and placed in the golden vase in the presence of the four Grand Law protectors. Living Buddhas of great learning will be invited to read sutras for seven days. Then under the supervision of all the Living Buddhas jointly with the *amban*, the imperial representative, a grand religious ceremony for selecting the incarnation will be conducted in front of Sakyamuni's statue in Jokhang Temple, and one of the tablets will be drawn from the vase, thus deciding the succession of the new Living Buddha. The soul boys of the Dalai Lama and Panchen Erdeni also will go through the same procedures. In case only one soul boy is picked up, his tablet also will be put into the vase along with a blank one. If the blank tablet is drawn, this soul boy will not be chosen. A further search will be made. The golden vase will be placed before the Tsong-kha-pa's statue and be taken care of, and sacrifices will be made to it. All these are done by the Great Emperor's order to bring about prosperity for the Yellow Sect and to avoid

possible trickeries which might be employed by the Law protectors.

2. Foreign travellers and traders have to abide by Tibetan laws and customs. The records of their names shall be submitted to the *amban*. The frequency of their visits and the duration of their stay are restricted. Nepalese traders are permitted to come to Tibet three times a year, and those from Kashmir once a year. Foreigners will enter and leave by the appointed outposts of Rgyal-rtse and Ding-ri, where they must show their passports for inspection. Foreigners who apply for entering Lhasa shall submit their application to the *rdzong-dpon* in the border land and be subject to inspection by the Han officials (officials sent by the central government) at Rgyal-tse and Ding-ri before they are permitted to go to Lhasa. When they arrive at Lhasa, they shall be registered and inspected. Han officials or clerks who are found to have committed corruption or taken bribes must be punished. Those who come from Bhutan and Tze-mong-xiong (the old name for Sikkim) to Lhasa to arrange pilgrimage affairs shall report themselves to the authorities on arriving at Lhasa and be subject to inspection on leaving. Those sent by the Dalai Lama to Nepal to set up Buddhist statues or make pilgrimages to Buddhist stupas must obtain passports issued by the *amban* before leaving. If they can not return before the fixed time, the *amban* shall send documents to inform the king of the Gurkhas.

3. Most of the original Tibetan *zhangkas* (silver coins circulating in Tibet) were not minted with a sufficient amount of silver. Henceforth the new *zhangkas* shall be minted with Han silver (pure silver provided from interior areas). Counterfeiting is forbidden. Each new *zhangkas* has the Han characters "Treasure of Qian Long" in the centre of its face and the date of minting at the edge and the same in Tibetan on the back. According to the old rate of exchange, 6 *zhangkas* can be exchanged for 1 tael of Han silver. Each coin being 1.5 *qian* in

weight, six coins are 9 *qian* of silver in weight, so the difference of 1 *qian* may be taken as the charge of minting. The newly minted coins will be subject to inspection by the Han officials sent by the *amban*, jointly with *bka'-blon*. In the past, counterfeit *zhangkas* were minted in Nepal as well by the local government of Tibet. The rate of exchange for these coins is now stipulated as one hundred coins for 1 tael of Han silver. Further counterfeiting is forbidden. The rate of exchange of the *zhangkas* of sufficient silver minted in Nepal and Tibet is the same as mentioned above. If the new *zhangkas* are found to be minted with mixed metals, the *rtsis-dpon*, the monk officials and craftsmen entrusted by the Han officials and *bka'-blon* to do the work, will be severely punished by law and be fined twice the counterfeit coins they have minted.

4. Formerly, the Dbus and Gtsang regions had no regular army. The soldiers were recruited when necessary, so their combat effectiveness was quite low, and such recruitments created disturbances among the people. Now the Great Emperor has granted our request to organize a regular army of 3,000 men, of whom 1,000 will be stationed in the Dbus and the Gtsang region respectively and 500 will be stationed at Rgyal-rtse and Ding-ri respectively. The soldiers will be recruited from the main Tibetan areas. Every 500 soldiers will be under the command of a *mda'-dpon*. In the past, there were only five *mda'-dpon*. So the number of *mda'-dpon* will be increased according to the increased number of soldiers. The soldiers stationed at Lhasa will be under the command of the Lhasa military governor, while the soldiers stationed at Gzhis-kha-rtse, Rgyal-rtse, and Ding-ri will be under the command of the Gzhis-kha-rtse military governor. The name-list of the recruits shall be made in two copies: one will be submitted to the office of the *amban*, the other to the Bka'-shag. In the future, new recruits can be called up only to replenish the ranks when vacancies appear. All these soldiers are guards of the Dalai

Lama and the Panchen Erdeni.

5. According to the new military organization, under a *mda'-dpon* there are two *ru-dpon*, each commanding 250 soldiers; under a *ru-dpon* there are two *brgya-dpon*, each commanding 125 soldiers; under a *brgya-dpon* there are five *ding-dpon*, each commanding 25 soldiers. All these officers will be selected from capable young men and be appointed by the *amban* and the Dalai Lama, who will confirm the appointments with certificates. To fill a vacancy of a *mda'-dpon's* post, a *ru-dpon* will be promoted; to fill that of a *ru-dpon*, a *brgya-dpon* will be promoted. Servicemen of noble origin can only be promoted step by step, from *ding-dpon* to *brgya-dpon* and to higher ranks, and they cannot be promoted more than one grade at a time. In former times, commoners were not allowed to be promoted to a post higher than *ding-dpon*. From now on, they shall be promoted according to their knowledge, ability, and meritorious military service, and discrimination against them is not allowed. Those who violate military discipline will be punished severely.

6. In the past, the Tibetan soldiers were not provided with food and weapons. The soldiers had to provide themselves. When they ate the food up, they ran away. From now on, each soldier will be provided annually with 2 *dan* (a unit of dry measure for grain, equivalent to 1 hectolitre) and 5 *dou* (1 *dou*-1 decalitre) of grain. The total amount of provisions for the army will be 7,500 *dan* of grain. To provide grain for the army only by means of farmland tax collected from the Dbus and Gtsang regions will not be sufficient, so the products of the farms of Zhwa-dmar-pa grom-pa huthugthu and the products from the five farms presented by Mi-'gyur bsod-nams dpal-'byor, the son of Bstan-'dzin dpal-byor, totally 3,170 *dan* of grain, will be used as army provisions. And the property of Zhwa-dmar-pa blo-bzang rgyal-ban will be sold to make up the difference.

The Dalai Lama will confer on the recruits corvée-free certificates to enhance their military pride. As to the salaries for the officers, *mda'-dpon* will not receive salary, because they have been bestowed manorial estates by the Dalai Lama. The annual salaries for the *ru-dpon, brgya-dpon,* and *ding-dpon* will be 36 taels, 20 taels, and 14.8 taels of silver respectively, totally 2,688 taels of silver, which will be provided by the Tibetan government to the *amban,* who then will give out the officers' pay twice a year, in spring and autumn. The soldiers' provisions will be given out by the *mda'-dpon* and brgya-dpon, also twice a year, in spring and autumn. Any shortness of pay will not be allowed.

7. As to weapons, 50 percent of the soldiers will use firearms, 30 percent bows and arrows, and 20 percent knives and spears. The surplus weapons in the monasteries in the Dbus and the Gtsang regions will be bought by the Tibetan government. The expenses will be paid from the 550 taels of silver got by selling yak butter, an income from Zhwa-dmar-pa's pastureland confiscated by the government. Annualy, the local government will have bows, arrows, and gunpowder made in Kong-po and Bian-ba. The soldiers shall practise military exercises regularly.

8. In the past, the revenue and expenditure of the Dalai Lama and Panchen Erdeni were not subject to the supervision of the *amban.* As the Dalai Lama and Panchen Erdeni engaged in religious affairs wholeheartedly and paid little attention to financial details, their financial affairs were left in the hands of their relatives and attendants; under such circumstances fraudulent practices were hard to avoid. By the Great Emperor's order, the *amban* shall check their accounts and submit a report to the Emperor twice a year, in the spring and autumn seasons. Anyone who practises irregularities will be punished.

9. Considering that the Tibetan people suffered much from the recent invasion of the Gurkhas, who razed many villages to the ground, the government determines to exempt the Rje-drung, Rongshia, and Gnya'lam areas from two years' corvée and taxes; the Tzongke, Ding-ri, Kha-dui, and Chong-dui areas

from one year's corvée and taxes; the Dbus and Gtsang regions from the taxes unpaid before the Iron Pig year; and, finally, all the government officials, monk or lay, and the heads of all the *rdzong* and *chol* from half of the taxes unpaid by them. All these measures conform to the imperial decree of taking good cares of the Tibetan people.

10. The *amban* is equal in status with the Dalai Lama and Panchen Erdeni, and they will handle political affairs through consultation with each other. All the officials of the local government of Tibet, from the *bka'-blon* down, including all the Living Buddhas, are subordinated to the *amban*. Before Panchen Erdeni's coming of age, all the affairs of the Bkra-shis-lhun-po Monastery will be managed by the Bsod-dpon mkhan-po. In order to settle all important affairs justly, he shall submit a report about them to the *amban* beforehand, so that the *amban* may handle them on his tour of inspection there.

11. In order to fill a vacancy of a *bka'-blon*'s post, the *amban* and the Dalai Lama will nominate jointly two candidates from *mda'-dpon, rtsis-dpon*, or *phyag-mdzod* according to their ability and merits, and the Great Emperor will appoint one of them *bka'-blon*. The candidate for the lama *bka'-blon* will be nominated from major *mkhan-po*. The candidate for a *mda'-dpon* will be nominated from *ru-dpon,* or *rdzong-dpon* in border areas. The candidate for a *rtsis-dpon* or *phyag-mdzod* will be nominated from *gnyer-tshang-pa, gsher-dpang* (judges), senior secretaries of the Bka'-shag or *rtsis-grom* lamas (monk officials). The vacancy of *gnyer-tshang-pa* or *gsher-dpang* will be filled by a nominee from *Zhol-sde-pa*, Lhasa *mo-dpon*, or *mda'-dpon*. The vacancy of *Zhol-sde-pa*, Lhasa *mo-dpon*, or *mda'-dpon* will be filled by a nominee from *rdzong-dpon* or Bka'-shag *grom-ni* (reception personnel of the Bka'-shag). The monk officials in the offices of *gnyer-tshang-pa* and *Zhol-sde-pa* will be nominated from the lamas of big monasteries. The senior secretary will be nominated from junior secretaries or Bka'-shag *grom-ni*. The *rdzong-*

dpon of a big *rdzong* or a borderland *rdzong* will be nominated from the *rdzong-dpon* of small *rdzong*. The junior secretary will be nominated from *brgya-dpon* in military service or other appropriate persons. The *rdzong-dpon* of a small *rdzong* or a borderland *rdzong* will be nominated from ordinary clerks.

In former times, the lama *rdzong-dpon* of various *rdzong* were nominated from among the Dalai Lama's attendants. Most of them could not assume the posts themselves and thus sent their agents to the posts instead. Such people often indulged in corruption and blackmail. Hereafter, these agents will be appointed by the *amban,* not by *ersis-grom* lamas. The junior secretaries and *grom-ni* of the Bka'-shag, though low in status, are very important, for they work by the side of *bka'-blon*. They will be nominated from competent lay officials.

The management of the mint has been recently reorganized, and two *rtsis-dpon* and two *rtsis-grom* have been appointed its directors. In the future when their posts become vacant, the successors will be appointed by the *amban* and the Dalai Lama through negotiation. Except for *bka'-blon* and *mda'-dpon*, who will be appointed by the Emperor, all the civil and military officials will be appointed by the *amban* and the Dalai Lama, who will confirm their appointments with certificates written in Manchu, Han, and Tibetan scripts. The officials below the status of *bka'-blon* and *mda'-dpon* will be promoted according to the regulations mentioned above. Violation will not be allowed. The administrators in charge of fodder, of *zanba* (barley cakes), and of tents, as well as guards, will be appointed by the Dalai Lama himself, for they are not important.

In the past, there were no stipulations about the number and promotion of monk officials in the Bkra-shis-lhun-po Monastery. Hereafter, a *phyag-mdzod* lama will be nominated from *bsod-dpon* lamas (the chiefs in charge of diet) or *gzim-dpon* lamas (the chiefs in charge of dormitories). The vacancy of *bsod-dpon* will be filled by a nominee from *rtsis-grom* lamas. The vacancy of *gzim-dpon* will be filled by a nominee from *grom-ni* (attendants). Under the jurisdiction of the Bkra-shis-lhun-po Monastery there are only a few villages, and the *rdzong* and *chol* in its border areas are not important ones; nevertheless, the *phyag-mdzod, bsod-dpon, gzim-dpon, rdzong-dpon,* and other officials will be appointed by the Panchen Erdeni and the *amban* through consultation according to the regulations concerning the Dbus region. Such junior personnel as those in charge of butter, *zanba*, and firewood will be appointed by Panchen Erdeni himself according to their ability and skills. The *ula* service may be allocated to the people according to the old regulations.

12. In former times, the attendant officials of the Dalai Lama and Panchen Erdeni were appointed from among their relatives. For instance, Dalai Lama's uncle and Panchen Erdeni's father, Dpal-ldan don-grub, were appointed officials without authorization; and Dalai Lama's brother Blo-bzang dge-deng gyur-pa indulged in unlawful practices, relying on powerful connections. Henceforth, according to the wishes of Tibetan lay people and monks of all ranks, including the monks and lay persons in Bkra-shis-lhun-po, while the Dalai Lama and Panchen Erdeni are alive, their relatives will not be allowed to participate in government and political affairs. After they have passed away, their relatives can be appointed to appropriate posts according to their abilities.

13. In spring and autumn, the *amban* will make tours of inspection twice a year round the Dbus-Gtsang region and review the troops there. At that time, any complaints against Han officials or *rdzong-dpon* about their bullying and exploiting the people may be submitted to the *amban* for investigation and ascertainment. During his tour, all the labour services done for the *amban* must be paid in order to lighten the local people's economic burden.

14. Tibet borders on Nepal, Bhutan, and Sikkim. In former

times, envoys were sent from those countries to Tibet to offer tributes or arrange public affairs. Due to the unsuitable forms and formulas of letters written by the Dalai Lama, and for other reasons, there were frequent disputes between Tibet and those bordering countries. For instance, the government of Nepal once sent to the Tibetan authorities an official letter on the problem about the Tibetan *zhangkas*. The Tibetan authorities dealt with it carelessly. This led to a battle between Tibet and Nepal, though later the Nepalese government showed signs of repenting its errors and made allegiance to our country. From now on, when Nepal sends its messengers to meet the Dalai Lama and the *amban*, the reply must be written according to the *amban's* instruction and all the tributes offered by foreigners also shall be subject to his inspection. The management of foreign affairs involving Tibetan borders must be concentrated in the hands of the *amban*.

The king of Bhutan, on whom the Emperor has bestowed an honorific title, pays tributes to the Dalai Lama and Panchen Erdeni annually, though he adheres to a different religion. Sikkim, Rdzong-pa, Mon-tang, and other tributaries also pay tributes. No tributes shall be refused, but shall be submitted to the *amban* for inspection. When foreigners enter Tibet, the *rdzong-dpon* of the border *rdzong* shall register their number and report to the *amban*, and they shall be examined by the Han officials at Rgyal-rtse and Ding-ri before they are permitted to go to Lhasa. The correspondence from tributary states to the Dalai Lama and the Panchen Erdeni shall be translated and submitted to the *amban*, who then will undertake to give appropriate replies for the grand lamas. The correspondence sent to *bka'-blon* from abroad must be submitted to the *amban* and Dalai Lama, who then will undertake to reply for the *bka'-blon*. Any private correspondence between *bka'-blon* and foreign countries is forbidden. All the above-mentioned regulations involving foreign affairs shall be observed strictly.

15. The Tibetan areas of Rje-drung, Gnya'lam, Rongshia, Kha-da, Sa-ga, and Khon-bu border on Nepal and are vital communication lines. Landmarks shall be set up at the Rje-ban bridge in Rje-drung, at the Pan-zhan iron bridge in Gnya'lam, and along the borderline in Rongshia to restrict Nepalese traders and Tibetans from crossing the border at discretion. On his inspection tour, the *amban* shall make a survey of the landmarks. Therefore, where the landmarks are needed, there they should be set up immediately. Any delay may result in disputes with other countries.

16. The border areas are contiguous to foreign countries, so it is very important to administer properly affairs concerning the local people there and inspect the travellers. Formerly, most of the competent *rdzong-dpon* were sent to work in Lhasa, but the incapable ones were sent to the border *rdzong*. Such a practice is not good for administration. From now on, the *rdzong-dpon* in the borderland shall be promoted from the *rdzong-dpon* of small *rdzong* or the captains in the army. After a period of three years, their work will be checked by their higher authorities. If they work well, they will be nominated as candidates for *mda'-dpon*. Otherwise they will be removed.

17. In the past, only aristocrats could be appointed as officials and officers, while the commoners could not. Hereafter, if a common soldier is competent and combat-worthy, though not of noble origin, he may be appointed as *ding-dpon*, and even be promoted step by step to *mda'-dpon*. As to official posts other than military, only aristocrats may be appointed according to the old regulations. But before an aristocrat comes of age, he is not fit to take an official post. So a young man of noble origin can be appointed to the post of junior secretary, Bka'-shag *grom-ni*, or *rdzong-dpon* of a small *rdzong* only after he has reached 18 years of age.

18. The *mkhan-po* is the chief of a monastery, so he should be a man of great learning and good behavior. Nevertheless, the

recent investigations have revealed that most of the Living Buddhas of the big monasteries are unqualified for their religious posts, because they possess a large number of manorial estates and receive a great amount of donations and tributes due to their high prestige among the people. In addition, they engage in commercial activities, becoming greedy and insatiably avaricious. Hereafter, the Living Buddhas of big monasteries will be appointed by the Dalai Lama, the *amban* and Rje-drung Huthugthu through consultation, who then will confirm the appointments with certificates under their seals. As to the *mkhan-po* and Living Buddhas of small monasteries, they will be appointed by the Dalai Lama according to the old regulations.

19. When taxes are paid with silver coins instead of material objects, the Tibetan coins, old or new, will be converted according to their respective ratio of exchange. Overtax is forbidden. When official clerks make purchases, they must deal fairly with merchants and traders, so that the latter will not suffer from any unjust bargains.

20. The import and export taxes on rice, salt, and other goods will be levied at Rje-drung and Gnya'lam according to the old regulations. An increase of taxes by the local government will not be allowed without the *amban*'s permission.

21. In the past, various corvée and taxes were allocated almost only to the poor people. Rich families, the Dalai Lama's relatives, the grand Huthugthu's relatives, most of the farmers on the manorial estates of *kha'-blons*, *mda'-dpon*, and the grand Living Buddhas—all received corvée-free certificates issued by the Dalai Lama and the Panchen Erdeni. From now on, all the corvée-free certificates will be withdrawn so that the corvée may be shouldered equally by all the Tibetan people. On those who should be given special treatment for their merits the corvée-free certificates will be conferred by the Dalai Lama and the *amban* after consultation. All the soldiers of the newly organ-

ized Tibetan troops will be given corvée-free certificates according to the name-list, and the certificates will be withdrawn when they have died or left the army.

22. The name-lists of all the Living Buddhas and lamas in the monasteries under the jurisdiction of the Dalai Lama and the name-lists of the residents in the villages where the Huthugthus come from shall be made by *bka'-blon* and submitted to the *amban* and the Dalai Lama for their inspection. If a lama is found travelling without a passport, the chiefs of his monastery such as the *mkhan-po* and the *dza-sag* will be subject to punishment.

23. The Mongol princes in Qinghai often invite Living Buddhas of great learning to read sutras at their homes. Some have invited the high-ranking lamas through the *amban*, but others have not. So it has often been difficult to find out the Living Buddhas' whereabouts. From now on, when Mongol princes invite Tibetan Living Buddhas, they shall submit a report to the Xining governor, and the latter will send a document to the *amban*, who then will issue passports to the lamas permitted to leave and at the same time inform the Xining governor for his reference. The Living Buddha who plans to leave Tibet for other places to make a pilgrimage also has to apply for a passport before leaving. Otherwise, the *mkhan-po* and other chiefs of his monastery shall be punished.

24. According to old regulations, the *ula* service was assigned to the local people by means of certificates issued by the Dalai Lama, but many malpractices arose out of this system. For instance, the relatives of *bka'-blon*, *mda'-dpon*, and the Dalai Lama assigned *ula* services to the people without authorization for the purpose of transporting grain and other materials. From now on, the Living Buddhas and other religious chiefs cannot enjoy *ula* services during their tour on private affairs, but on public errands they may enjoy the *ula* on their journey with the certificates issued by and affixed with the seals of the

amban and the Dalai Lama.

25. Cases of scuffle, murder, and burglary may be handled according to the old regulations, but they should be handled fairly and justly in the light of law. Recently the *bka'-blon* and *rnang-rtse-shag mi-dpon* (head of the police of Lhasa) have not only handled the cases unfairly, but imposed on the convicts undue fines (gold, silver, cattle, or sheep) which they did not hand over to the government but pocketed for themselves. Some of the *bka'-blon* even framed people of low status and asked the Dalai Lama to confiscate their properties. From now on, the fines imposed on the convicts will be registered and handed over to the *amban's* office. All court decisions shall be submitted to the *amban* for examination and approval. Any lawsuit, no matter who is involved, must be handled fairly according to the law. If a *bka'-blon* is found to have occupied the people's properties, he will be removed from his office, his property will be confiscated, and the properties occupied by him will be returned to the original owners.

26. Ammunition for the drilling of troops will be made under the supervision of the Bka'-shag annually in the region of Kong-po, then transported to Lhasa and distributed to the troops. Due to the fact that the troops in the Gtsang region have no cannons, two of the fourteen newly made cannons will be set aside for the troops in the Gtsang region, and the rest will be allocated to the Dalai Lama's troops.

27. In the past, when a *bka'-blon* or *mda'-dpon* assumed his post, the Dalai Lama would assign him residences and manorial estates, but on leaving the office, he had to return those properties to the government. It was found recently that some *bka'-blon* and *mda'-dpon* who had left their official post did not return the properties assigned, but let their family members continue to occupy them. The result is that the government had to assign other residences and manorial estates to newly appointed *bka'-blon* and *mda'-dpon*. Hereafter, on leaving the

office, *bka'-blon* and *mda'-dpon* must hand over those properties to the newly appointed ones and should not occupy them as their own.

28. According to the old regulations, the wages of the lamas and Living Buddhas should be paid on fixed dates of the year. But recently it was found that they have always been paid ahead of schedule. Hereafter, their wages should be paid at the fixed dates and should never be paid ahead of time. The Rje-drung Huthugthu must look into the matter and punish those who do not pay them in due time or in due amount.

29. In order to collect taxes and land-rents, the local government usually sent monk officials to the nearby villages and lay officials to the farther villages. A recent investigation revealed that there were a few bad elements among the monk and lay officials and *rdzong-dpon*, who pocketed the taxes, rents, and articles for themselves instead of handing them over to the government. They even collected taxes and rents ahead of time, some of the taxes not being due until the next year. They even imposed on other villagers the taxes due to be paid by families who had fled. As a result, taxes have become a very heavy burden on the local people and they are living in dire poverty. Hereafter, the collection of taxes or rents in advance is forbidden. The taxes and rents due to be paid by families who have fled will be exempted temporarily. They shall be paid off by the runaway families when they come back.

[The fifty-eighth year of the reign of Emperor Qian Long (1793)]

APPENDIX C

The Agreement of the Central People's Government and the Local Government of Tibet on Measures for the Peaceful Liberation of Tibet

This historic agreement bringing about the peaceful liberation of Tibet was signed in Peking [Beijing] on May 23, 1951, in the former Imperial Palace. The full text follows.

The Tibetan nationality is one of the nationalities with a long history within the boundaries of China and, like many other nationalities, it has performed its glorious duty in the course of the creation and development of our great Motherland. But over the last one hundred years or more, imperialist forces penetrated into China, and in consequence also penetrated into the Tibetan region and carried out all kinds of deceptions and provocations. Like previous reactionary governments, the Kuomintang reactionary government continued to carry out a policy of oppressing and sowing dissension among the nationalities, causing division and disunity among the Tibetan people. And the Local Government of Tibet did not oppose the imperialist deceptions and provocations, and adopted an unpatriotic attitude towards our great Montherland. Under such conditions, the Tibetan nationality and people were plunged into the depths of enslavement and suffering.

In 1949, basic victory was achieved on a nationwide scale in the Chinese People's War of Liberation; the common domestic enemy of all nationalities—the Kuomintang reactionary government—was overthrown; and the common foreign enemy of all the nationalities—the aggressive imperialist forces—was driven out. On this basis, the founding of the People's Republic of China and of the Central People's Government was announced. In accordance with the *Common Programme* passed by the Chinese People's Political Consultative Conference, the Central People's Government declared that all nationalities within the boundaries of the People's Republic of China are equal, and that they shall establish unity and mutual aid and oppose imperialism and their own public enemies, so that the People's Republic of China will become a big fraternal and cooperative family, composed of all its nationalities; that within the big family of all nationalities of the People's Republic of China, national regional autonomy shall be exercised in areas where national minorities are concentrated, and all national minorities shall have freedom to develop their spoken and written languages and to preserve or reform their customs, habits, and religious beliefs, while the Central People's Government shall assist all national minorities to develop their political, economic, cultural, and educational construction work. Since then, all nationalities within the country, with the exception of those in the areas of Tibet and Taiwan, have gained liberation. Under the unified leadership of the Central People's Government and the direct leadership of higher levels of People's Governments, all national minorities are fully enjoying the right of national equality and have established, or are establishing, national regional autonomy.

In order that the influences of aggressive imperialist forces in Tibet might be successfully eliminated, the unification of the territory and sovereignty of the People's Republic of China accomplished, and national defence safeguarded; in order that the tibetan nationality and people might be freed and return to the big family of the People's Republic of China to enjoy the same rights of national equality as all the other nationalities in the country and develop their political, economic, cultural, and educational work, the Central People's Government, when it ordered the People's Liberation Army to march into Tibet, notified the Local Government of Tibet to send delegates to the central authorities to conduct talks for the conclusion of and agreement on measures for the peaceful liberation of Tibet.

In the latter part of April 1951, the delegates with full powers of the Local Government of Tibet arrived in Peking. The Central People's Government appointed representatives with full powers to conduct talks on a friendly basis with the delegates with full powers of the Local Government of Tibet. As a result of these talks, both parties agreed to conclude this agreement and guarantee that it will be carried into effect.

1. The Tibetan people shall unite and drive out imperialist aggressive forces from Tibet; the Tibetan people shall return to the big family of the Motherland—the People's Republic of China.

2. The Local Government of Tibet shall actively assist the People's Liberation Army to enter Tibet and consolidate the national defence.

3. In accordance with the policy towards nationalities laid down in the *Common Programme of the Chinese People's Political Consultative Conference* the Tibetan people have the right of exercising national regional autonomy under the unified leadership of the Central People's Government.

4. The central authorities will not alter the existing political system in Tibet. The central authorities also will not alter the established status, functions, and powers of the Dalai Lama. Officials of various ranks shall hold office as usual.

5. The established status, functions, and powers of the Panchen Ngoerhtehni shall be maintained.

6. By the established status, functions, and powers of the Dalai Lama and of the Panchen Ngoerhtehni are meant the status, functions, and powers of the thirteenth Dalai Lama and of the ninth Panchen Ngoerhtehni when they were in friendly and amicable relations with each other.

7. The policy of freedom of religious belief laid down in the *Common Programme of the Chinese People's Political Consultative Conference* shall be carried out. The religious beliefs, customs, and habits of the Tibetan people shall be respected, and lama monasteries shall be protected. The central authorities will not effect a change in the income of the monasteries.

8. Tibetan troops shall be reorganized by stages into the People's Liberation Army, and become a part of the national defence forces of the People's Republic of China.

9. The spoken and wirtten language and school education of the Tibetan nationality shall be developed step by step in accordance with the actual conditions in Tibet.

10. Tibetan agriculture, livestock raising, industry, and commerce shall be developed step by step, and the people's livelihood shall be improved step by step in accordance with the actual conditions in Tibet.

11. In matters related to various reforms in Tibet, there will be no compulsion on the part of the central authorities. The Local Government of Tibet should carry out reforms of its own accord, and when the people raise demands for reform, they shall be settled by means of consultation with the leading personnel of Tibet.

12. Insofar as former pro-imperialist and pro-Kuomintang officials resolutely sever relations with imperialism and the Kuomintang and do not engage in sabotage or resistance, they may continue to hold office irrespective of their past.

13. The People's Liberation Army entering Tibet shall abide by all the above-mentioned policies and shall also be fair in all buying and selling and shall not arbitrarily take a single needle or thread from the people.

14. The Central People's Government shall conduct the centralized handling of all external affairs of the area of Tibet; and there will be peaceful coexistence with neighbouring countries and establishment and development of fair commercial and

trading relations with them on the basis of equality, mutual benefit, and mutual respect for territory and sovereignty.

15. In order to ensure the implementation of this agreement, the Central People's Government shall set up a military and administrative committee and a military area headquarters in Tibet and apart from the personnel sent there by the Central People's Government shall absorb as many local Tibetan personnel as possible to take part in the work.

Local Tibetan personnel taking part in the military and administrative committee may include patriotic elements from the Local Government of Tibet, various districts, and leading monasteries; the name-list shall be drawn up after consultation between the representatives designated by the Central People's Government and the various quarters concerned and shall be submitted to the Central People's Government for appointment.

16. Funds needed by the military and administrative committee, the military area headquarters, and the People's Liberation Army entering Tibet shall be provided by the Central People's Government. The Local Government of Tibet will assist the People's Libertion Army in the purchase and transport of food, fodder, and other daily necessities.

17. This agreement shall come into force immediately after signatures and seals are affixed to it.

Signed and sealed by:
Delegates with full powers of the Central People's Government:
Chief Delegate: *Li Wei-han*
Delegates: *Zhang Jing-wu*
        Zhang Guo-hua
        Sun Zhi-yuan
Delegates with full powers of the Local Government of Tibet:
Chief Delegate: *Kaloon Ngabou Ngawang Jigme*
Delegates: *Dzasak Khemey Sonam Wangdi*
        Khentrung Thupten Tenthar

Khenchung Thupten Lekmuun
Rimshi Samposey Tenzin Thundup

Peking, May 23, 1951.

论西藏政教合一制度

东嘎·洛桑赤列

*

外文出版社出版

（中国北京百万庄路 24 号）

邮政编码 100037

北京外文印刷厂印刷

1991 年（大 32 开）第一版

1993 年第二次印刷

（英）

ISBN 7—119—00672—X /Z·252（外）

00800